© Copyright, 1992, by William J. Maitland

All rights reserved. No part of this book may be reproduced in any form or by electronic or mechanical means including information storage and retrieval systems without permission in writing from the publisher, except by a reviewer, who may quote brief passages in a review.

Library of Congress Catalog Card Number 91-91263

COVER PHOTO: by William J. Maitland, © Copyright 1992
ILLUSTRATIONS: by William J. Maitland, © Copyright 1992
PHOTOS: by William J. Maitland © Copyright 1992

YOUNG BALLPLAYER IN DODGERS UNIFORM: Matthew Barclay
YOUNG BALLPLAYER IN "A's" UNIFORM: Jesse Romans

Printed and bound in the United States of America.
Published in the United States by:
MAITLAND ENTERPRISES PUBLISHING
8118 NORTH 28TH AVENUE
PHOENIX, ARIZONA 85051-6307

ISBN Number 0-936759-14-3

PUBLISHED BY: Maitland Enterprises, 8118 North 28th Avenue, Phoenix, AZ 85051
COVER PHOTO BY: William J. Maitland, © copyright 1992
ILLUSTRATIONS BY: William J. Maitland, © Copyright 1992
PHOTOS BY: William J. Maitland, © Copyright 1992

TYPESETTING BY Professional Scribe, Phoenix, Arizona
COVER DESIGN BY: Terri Macdonald
EDITED BY: Mary Hawkins and William J. Maitland

YOUNG BALLPLAYER IN DODGERS UNIFORM: Matthew Barclay
YOUNG BALLPLAYER IN "A's" UNIFORM: Jesse Romans

Library of Congress Cataloging in Publication Data
Maitland, William J. Library of Congress Catalog Number 89-90833
Young Ballplayers Guide to Safe Pitching - AGES 8 THRU ADULT - PROGRAM II
ISBN 0-9336759-14-3

Young Ballplayers Guide to Safe Pitching - AGES 8 THRU ADULT.
©Copyright 1992 by William J. Maitland. Printed and bound in the United States of America. All rights reserved. No part of this book may be reproduced in any form or by electronic or mechanical means including information storage and retrieval systems without permission in writing from the publisher, except by a reviewer, who may quote brief passages in a review.

YOUNG BALLPLAYER'S GUIDE TO: SAFE PITCHING

AGES EIGHT through ADULT

with conditioning and weight training to develop power throwing and batting

PROGRAM II

By William J. Maitland

Published by:
MAITLAND ENTERPRISES

8118 NORTH 28TH AVENUE
PHOENIX, ARIZONA 85051-6307

DEDICATION

This book is dedicated to the parents, coaches, and trainers who devote their time to safe training of young boys and girls involved in recreational and athletic activities. It is dedicated to the principal of drug free training and drug free life styles and to those children and adults who espouse the natural high of athletic activity and conditioning.

The author expresses his appreciation for the cooperation of the mother of Jesse Romans, Dorothy Romans, as well as the parents of Matthew Barclay, Mr. and Mrs. John Barclay.

Coach Maitland has had the pleasure of coaching a Little League team with John Barclay where the fine tuning of the methods discussed in this book took place.

TABLE OF CONTENTS

	PAGE
DISCLAIMER	i
PREFACE	ii

CHAPTER 1

REASON FOR CONCENTRATION PITCHING	1
SHAVING BODY MOVEMENTS IS SHAVING ERRORS	2

CHAPTER 2

MUSCLE DIAGRAM - ILLUSTRATION	4-5
SKELETAL SYSTEM DIAGRAM ILLUSTRATION	6
BODY MOTION = SPEED	7
PRODUCING TORQUE	9

CHAPTER III

EPIPHYSIS: KEY TO PITCHING ARM LIFE	10
FINGER PRESSURE = BALL MOVEMENT	12
CURVEBALL ARM HARM	13
IMAGINED DELIVERY OF CURVEBALL	14
ACTUAL DELIVERY OF CURVEBALL	15
ENGINEERING AND PHYSIOLOGY	15

CHAPTER IV

NEW DELIVERY	16

CHAPTER V

TEACHING SAFE THROWING AT THE ELEMENTARY LEVEL	19

CHAPTER VI
THINKING PITCHER-CRUCIAL TO THE GAME	21
PONY LEAGUES-PLAN PITCHES BEFORE GAMES	23
TEACHING MIND CONTROL	24

CHAPTER VII
CATCHER FOR THE DEFENSE	26

CHAPTER VIII
LACK OF FIELD TIME IN LITTLE LEAGUE?	28

CHAPTER IX
MAKE IT HARD TO HIT	30
DISCUSSION OF PROBLEMS AND TACTICS	31
DRILL FOR BODY COORDINATION IN THROWING	32

CHAPTER X
MOST IMPORTANT PITCH	33
FAST BALL GRIPS	34
SINKING FAST BALL	36
VARIATIONS OF THE CHANGE UP PITCH	37

CHAPTER XI
PITCHES FOR ADVANCED TRAINEES	38
THE SLIDER	40

CHAPTER XII
RELIEF PITCHES	42
SPLIT FINGER FAST BALL	42
THE KNUCKLE BALL	43
IMPORTANCE OF THE CHANGE UP	44

CHAPTER XIII
RESTING THE TOTAL ATHLETE	45
BODY FATIGUE IN PITCHING	46
ORGANIZED YOUTH BASEBALL CAN PREVENT EXPERIENCE	46
PROLOG TO PITCHING SECTION	48

CHAPTER XIV

MUSCULAR DEVELOPMENT AND EMOTIONAL READINESS FOR COMPETITION	50
PROFILE OF DEVELOPMENT-AGE SEVEN	51
PROFILE OF DEVELOPMENT-AGE EIGHT	51
CONTINUUM OF SOCIALIZATION	52
PUBERTY AND THE CHANGE	52
AUTHOR'S PERSONAL OBSERVATIONS	52
CONCLUSION OF DEVELOPMENT CHAPTER	53
AUTHOR'S CAUTIONS AND RECOMMENDATIONS	53

CHAPTER XV

STRETCHES	55

CHAPTER XVI

WEIGHT TRAINING FOR PITCHERS AND BATTERS	67
WORKOUT DAY I – PROGRAM TWO	69
WORKOUT DAY II – PROGRAM TWO	81
WORKOUT DAY III – PROGRAM TWO	94

CHAPTER XVII

ARM THERAPY EXERCISES USED BY SPORTS CLINICS AND TRAINEEES	104
CHEAP TRAINING AIDS	107
CHARTS FOR WORKOUT PROGRESS RECORD	112

BIBLIOGRAPHY 116

INDEX 121

This author attempted to include the latest information available through research of the latest publications, seminars, training journals as well as his own experience in gaining knowledge through field coaching and participation in the activities described in this book. He has used this information to coach and train adults and children in safe, proper use of weights in an athletic or recreational mode in his program in Phoenix, Arizona, "MAITLAND SPORTS TRAINING". This program was founded in 1979 and has not had one complaint of injury as a result of the training method used in the program. This same information is contained in this book.

Continual research by practitioners and researchers in sports medicine and sports training cause many current training theories to be outdated or altered to assist the recreational and professional athlete achieve their goals of fitness and prowess on the field of play. This book is written in that spirit and the author and publisher or his affiliates assume no responsibility for injuries or any form of inconvenience physically or psychologically. THE READERS ARE CAUTIONED TO CONSULT WITH THEIR PHYSICIAN BEFORE EMBARKING ON ANY PHYSICAL TRAINING PROGRAM. THIS IS A TRAINING PROGRAM AND THE READERS ARE CAUTIONED TO BE WELL VERSED AND EXPERIENCED IN BEGINNING WEIGHT TRAINING PRIOR TO USING THIS PORTION OF THE PROGRAM. The book by the same author, *BEGINNING WEIGHT TRAINING FOR YOUNG ATHLETES—AGES 12 THRU ADULT:* can be ordered at the end of this book.

PREFACE

This book offers more than other baseball coaching-training books due to its direct discussion and basic presentation of skills and techniques for the amateur through professional player. Explicit, detailed photos show finger positions for safe, effective ball control on the pitch. The methods in this book have been discussed with ex-college and professional ball players who stated they wished they had someone to coach and train them in the beginning years — they felt their careers would have lasted longer.

The book educates the coaches, parents, and the trainees to the dangers hidden in the curveball and other "junk" pitches. Overzealous coaches and parents can cause life long harm to the young pitcher's arm by teaching the curveball and other "junk" pitches.

Defensive pitching is shown and discussed in detail to prevent injury from the batted ball after the pitch is delivered. Many young pitchers have had their promising careers interrupted or completely ruined by a batted ball to the knee or head.

Catchers, an important part of the pitching team, are taught techniques to take advantage of the youth league umpire's quirks in calling strikes.

Weight training for development of strength and speed in baseball throwing and hitting are shown and discussed in detail. Warm-ups and warm downs with proper stretching and relaxation methods are included in the total baseball training program.

Therapeutic exercises and strength enhancement for the wrist, shoulder, upper and lower arm and shoulder are specifically discussed and shown with equipment made from items found in the average home. Methods to improve hitting and throwing power are simply presented as part of the total body conditioning program.

Total body conditioning allows the ballplayer to use the entire body in the delivery of the pitch. This concentration of energy causes power in the throw with less injury to the epiphysis of the elbow. This growth area is very crucial to the health of the young pitcher and if caution is not practiced along with strength training and conditioning, serious harm can result. Ballplayers have become "has-beens" at age fourteen due to improper training by over zealous coaches or parents.

Baseball is a thinking person's game. The pitcher must be able to see the development of the play before it happens. In order to perform this task, his vision cannot be interrupted during the delivery of the pitch. The term introduced by the author of this book is *"point of concentration pitching."* This method allows the pitcher to deliver the pitch while never blocking the view to the "concentration point"...the catcher's glove.

The by-product of the "CONCENTRATION PITCH" is safety and total body involvement in each pitch. Since the vision is not blocked, the pitcher is not caught off guard when the ball is batted. Another advantage to the pitcher is the ability to go into the full stretch pitch without blocking the view between himself and the catcher. Subliminal factors are introduced to the art of pitching. We have now introduced the mind, by way of uninterrupted vision, to assist in the control of the pitch.

The greatest factor of all in coach Maitland's books is — injury prevention. His thirty years of training and coaching young athletes through adulthood are evident in all his works on coaching and training. Many of his former trainees are professional athletes or have received college scholarships for various sports including baseball. Those who chose other interests still maintain a healthy respect for health and fitness and continue their training throughout their adult life. They pass on the information learned at Maitland's Sports Training, the program where the trainees pictured in the books are trained and coached when not on the field of play.

Other books by William J. Maitland are, *Beginning Weight Training for Young Athletes — ages twelve through adult,* and the book for the next age group, *Weight Training for Gifted Athletes — ages fourteen through adult.* All the works stress safe training to ensure a long, injury free athletic, recreational, amateur or professional career.

Play it safe — Train to Maintain.

CHAPTER I

REASON FOR CONCENTRATION PITCHING

Many instructors/coaches have the young athlete do the overhead wind-up because everybody has done it since 1912. At the age of eighteen, I began to question the strict adherence to this practice. At that time, I was working for the East End YMCA in Painesville, Ohio, as a riding instructor and head counselor. There I played catcher for an exhibition by Bob Feller, formerly of the Cleveland Indians. Mr. Feller had just retired from baseball and was giving short demonstrations on his method of pitching.

When he went into his full wind-up I asked why he went overhead with his arms. He stated that this movement allowed him to move up the sleeves that were sticking to his arms. Since that July day I have had his comment in the back of my mind.

I had played a lot of sandlot ball in my day and caught for a lot of pitchers. I could see no reason why the movement overhead was necessary when I could throw the ball back without all the fanfare of the overhead wind-up.

When I began coaching baseball for elementary and junior high students, I noticed the young pitchers would imitate the movements as seen on television. I began realizing the youngsters would be off balance before delivery and had to recover their balance while trying to get the ball over the plate. They were, in fact, delivering the ball blind. They could not see the target but threw where they thought it should be. I wondered why more batters were not "harmed" as a result of this blind pitch.

SHAVING BODY MOVEMENTS SHAVES ERRORS

As the youngsters matured into junior high, they were able to balance better on the mound but seemed to tire quickly. I felt that if the body movements could be "shaved" to those necessary to effective delivery it would cut down on the energy exerted in delivery and provide a "longer life" of the arm for the pitcher.

I began experimenting with junior high school kids and found they became less confused in attempting to learn the importance of lower body strength in delivering the ball. They had a clear, uninterrupted view of the entire field before them which included the "point of concentration" — the catcher's glove.

The young pitcher became more relaxed and did not feel he was at the mercy of some strange, mysterious force that placed the ball over the plate. He did not block his vision twice as in the arms overhead method. He was less likely to place his stride foot over his pivot foot, thus increasing the chances for getting hit by the batted ball. Using the point of concentration pitching method allowed the youngster (male or female) to complete the pitch with an open stance while facing the batter for the defensive maneuver.

In this consideration of pitching methods, I found a fine book, "How To Throw A Curveball," written and demonstrated by Don Sutton, who pitched for the Los Angeles Dodgers for most of his career. In one passsage, Mr. Sutton states, "raising the arms is a good way to loosen your uniform and jersey so that your clothes do not bind on your arm when you are releasing the ball." Once again, I am reminded of my youth and Bob Feller's statement.

Mr. Sutton offers another observation in footwork. He states that in trying to get as much spin on the ball as he can, he finds that stepping over his left leg is more fluid than trying to stop. He states further that crossing over the pivot foot is a bad habit and should be eliminated. Mr. Sutton says too that it is an awkward position from which to field, and a line drive would be a disaster. He concludes that young players should practice ending the pitch with both feet square to the plate and their weight equally distributed.

I find it very difficult to retrain high school pitchers who are in my weight training program, Maitland Sports Training. Therefore, I attempt to enroll youngsters in my program before habits are ingrained and a false sense of security has developed.

I have a half brother who was permitted to quit high school to try out as a walk-on for the Chicago White Sox minor league team. His arm was hurt, and the continuous demand on the arm caused it to give out. The boy was given some rest. On his next attempt he was hit in the knee by a line drive to the mound. He never recovered from this experience. I hope everyone who reads this book can see more than the family ties to my concern for other young athletes of all sports and recreational programs. No youngsters should be pushed to satisfy the vicarious experiences of parents or coaches.

EXTENSOR CARPI
RADIALIS LONGUS

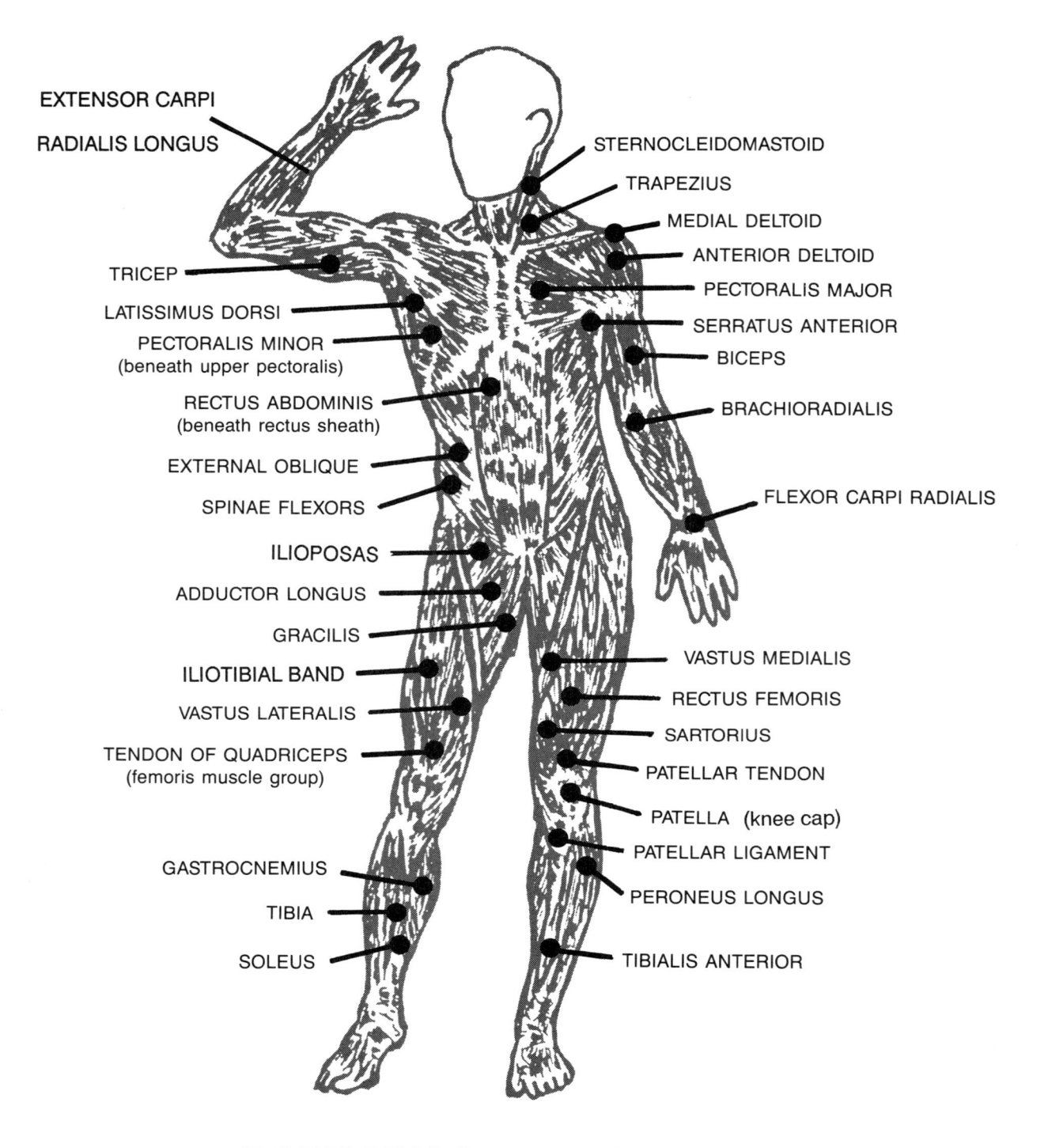

STERNOCLEIDOMASTOID
TRAPEZIUS
MEDIAL DELTOID
ANTERIOR DELTOID
PECTORALIS MAJOR
SERRATUS ANTERIOR
BICEPS
BRACHIORADIALIS

TRICEP
LATISSIMUS DORSI
PECTORALIS MINOR
(beneath upper pectoralis)
RECTUS ABDOMINIS
(beneath rectus sheath)
EXTERNAL OBLIQUE
SPINAE FLEXORS
ILIOPOSAS
ADDUCTOR LONGUS
GRACILIS
ILIOTIBIAL BAND
VASTUS LATERALIS
TENDON OF QUADRICEPS
(femoris muscle group)

FLEXOR CARPI RADIALIS

VASTUS MEDIALIS
RECTUS FEMORIS
SARTORIUS
PATELLAR TENDON
PATELLA (knee cap)
PATELLAR LIGAMENT
PERONEUS LONGUS

GASTROCNEMIUS
TIBIA
SOLEUS

TIBIALIS ANTERIOR

BODY MUSCLE DIAGRAM
ANTERIOR VIEW

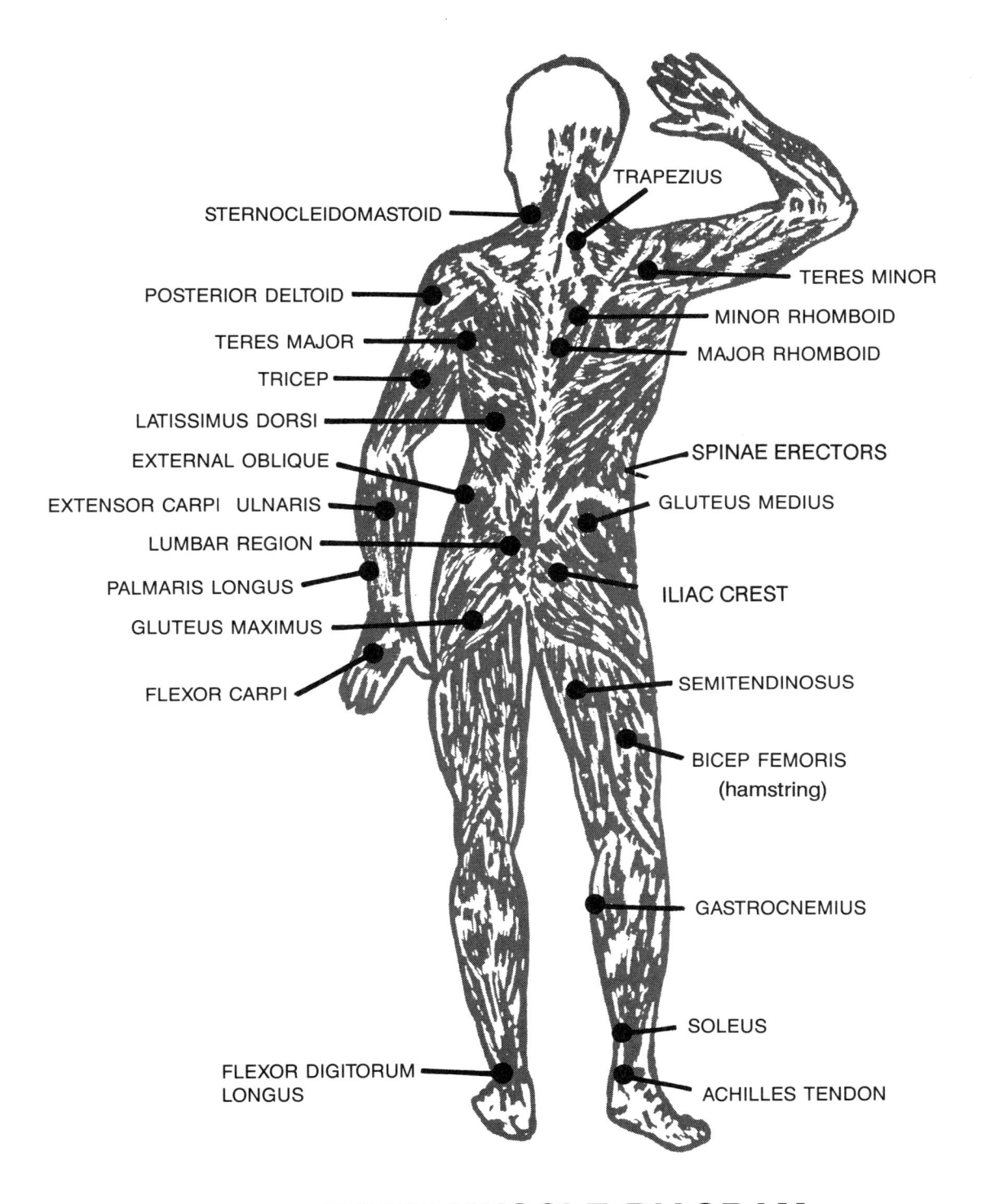

BODY MUSCLE DIAGRAM
POSTERIOR VIEW

- STERNOCLEIDOMASTOID
- TRAPEZIUS
- POSTERIOR DELTOID
- TERES MINOR
- MINOR RHOMBOID
- TERES MAJOR
- MAJOR RHOMBOID
- TRICEP
- LATISSIMUS DORSI
- SPINAE ERECTORS
- EXTERNAL OBLIQUE
- GLUTEUS MEDIUS
- EXTENSOR CARPI ULNARIS
- LUMBAR REGION
- PALMARIS LONGUS
- ILIAC CREST
- GLUTEUS MAXIMUS
- FLEXOR CARPI
- SEMITENDINOSUS
- BICEP FEMORIS (hamstring)
- GASTROCNEMIUS
- SOLEUS
- FLEXOR DIGITORUM LONGUS
- ACHILLES TENDON

SKELETAL SYSTEM

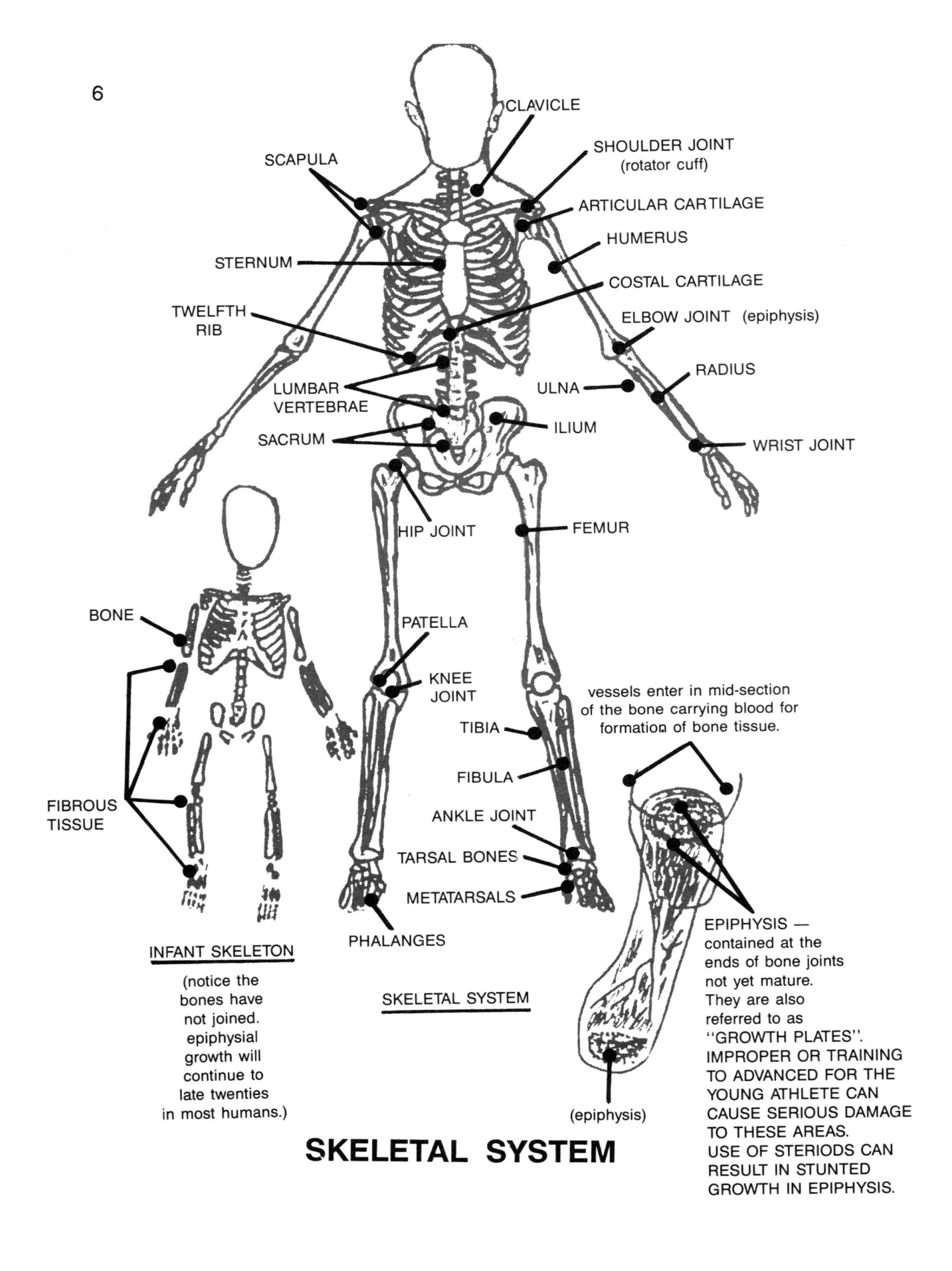

Labels on main skeleton:
- CLAVICLE
- SHOULDER JOINT (rotator cuff)
- SCAPULA
- ARTICULAR CARTILAGE
- HUMERUS
- STERNUM
- COSTAL CARTILAGE
- ELBOW JOINT (epiphysis)
- TWELFTH RIB
- RADIUS
- LUMBAR VERTEBRAE
- ULNA
- ILIUM
- SACRUM
- WRIST JOINT
- HIP JOINT
- FEMUR
- PATELLA
- KNEE JOINT
- TIBIA
- FIBULA
- ANKLE JOINT
- TARSAL BONES
- METATARSALS
- PHALANGES

SKELETAL SYSTEM

Infant Skeleton labels:
- BONE
- FIBROUS TISSUE

INFANT SKELETON
(notice the bones have not joined. epiphysial growth will continue to late twenties in most humans.)

vessels enter in mid-section of the bone carrying blood for formation of bone tissue.

(epiphysis)

EPIPHYSIS — contained at the ends of bone joints not yet mature. They are also referred to as "GROWTH PLATES". IMPROPER OR TRAINING TO ADVANCED FOR THE YOUNG ATHLETE CAN CAUSE SERIOUS DAMAGE TO THESE AREAS. USE OF STERIODS CAN RESULT IN STUNTED GROWTH IN EPIPHYSIS.

CHAPTER II

BODY MOTION = SPEED

Many articles and books refer to the motion by which torque is produced. Torque is that motion produced by a swift movement such as a whip that is snapped after being forced in an opposite direction. The speed of the "snap" at the end of the whip can surpass one hundred miles an hour easily.

In the article referred to in the Preface, Pat Jacobs of the N.S.C.A. states that the sequence of raising the arm overhead "does not directly contribute to the velocity of the pitch but may intensify the force produced by the musculature." Earlier, he says that the overhead wind-up "is recognized as creating a rhythm, relaxing the pitcher and perhaps confusing the batter."

I have talked to the young ballplayers with whom I work and found they experienced all of the above as described by Pat Jacobs. The youngsters had been trained to pitch at least one year prior to coming to my program. I introduced them to the point of concentration pitching (POCP). Initially they had problems coordinating the body parts to move forward rather than backward in the wind-up phase. The sequence is shown in the following pictures.

Figures 1a through 1c

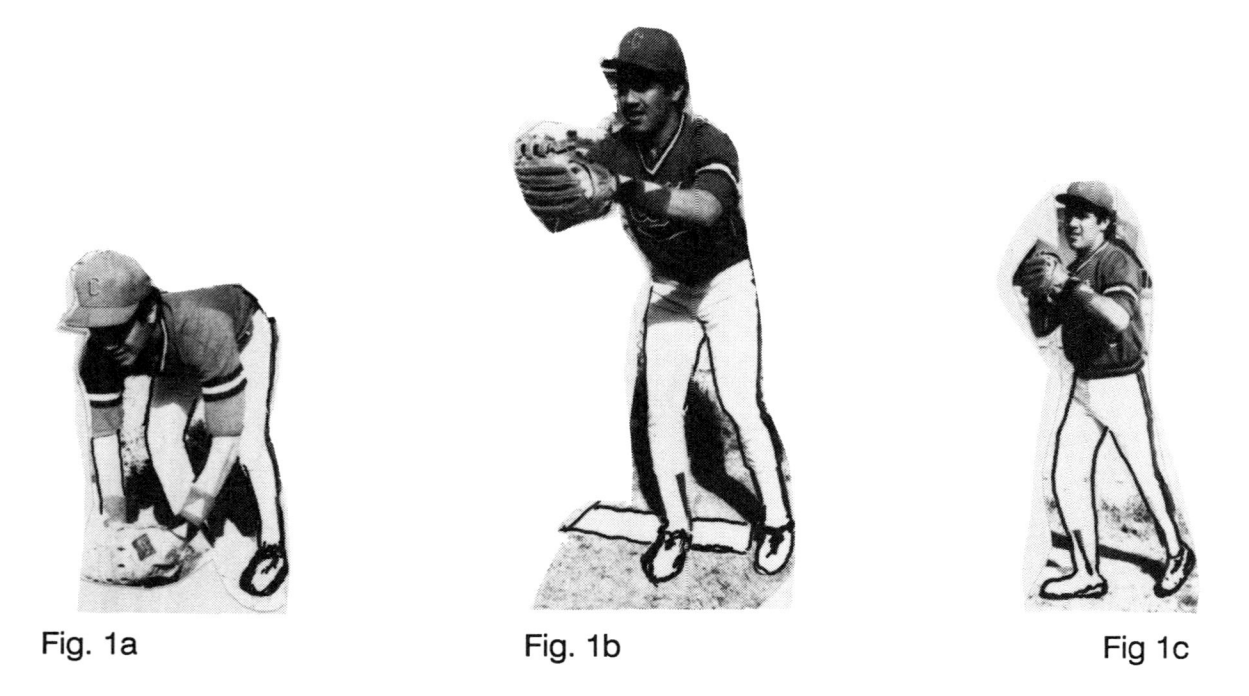

Fig. 1a

Fig. 1b

Fig 1c

Figures 1d through 1g

Fig. 1d

Fig 1e

Fig 1f

Fig 1g

Notice in the picture in Figure 1a, the pitcher is stretching laterally while his target is in full view. He also has a field of view that allows him to see any movement on the field. In this wind-up, the athlete uses the full weight of the deltoid (shoulder) complex while stretching his arms down and forward. This arm motion stretches the rectus abdominis, external obliques (stomach muscles) while permitting the lumbar region (lower back) of the spinal column to be stretched and relaxed. The torque is built up by the interplay of these regions of muscle as well as by the forced concentration and continued movement forward of the legs and torso.

Figures 1b, 1c, and 1d show the weight shifting from the front leg to be brought up to the midpoint of the stomach while the the pivot foot, having been placed on the rubber just behind the toes, moves in a pivotal fashion to the side of the foot, allowing for a strong push off the "cocked" leg while leaning forward. The muscles involved in these actions are numerous and are different only in the increased action by the stretching of the latissimus dorsi during the wind-up and the use of the strength from this region on delivery of the pitch.

Now see Figures 1f and 1g. The open stance is very important for the safety of the pitcher. This is demonstrated in Figure 1g.

See the diagrams following Chapter I for the location of the muscles mentioned. For further study of the muscles involved in pitching, see the literature cited in the Bibliography. I mention the effect of certain muscles which are used and stretched in the point of concentration pitching to show some similar actions and reactions of the muscles in the overhead as well as in the POCP method. I believe the POCP method is safer and delivers more consistent accuracy in the game. The youngster is able to pitch with less damage to the arm because of the decreased upward movement of the arm and decreased continual velocity from the strained rotator cuff (shoulder joint muscles).

Point of concentration pitching allows the delivery to come from a more stable grouping of muscles which youngsters need if they are to enjoy a long baseball life.

We will discuss the importance of the epiphysis (elbow) as well as potential damage to it in the next chapter.

CHAPTER III

EPIPHYSIS: KEY TO PITCHING ARM LIFE

Many people are not aware that the future of the young ballplayer can be ruined in one session by an overzealous parent/coach/instructor in Little League, Babe Ruth, Connie Mack, or any other organized youth baseball program. I have found that many overstrained, overworked youngsters who have shown promise at an early age such as ten, eleven, twelve, or thirteen, are "has-beens" by the time they reach "pony league' or "senior league" age.

I have my trainees warm up with a tennis ball prior to throwing the baseball. This tennis ball seems to force the trainee to use the entire body to throw the ball without shocking the arm with the centrifugal force of the baseball. It may sound overcautious, but I am very cautious with the arm of the aspiring pitcher, just as I was cautious of the legs of the race horses I used to train. After thirty or forty throws with the tennis ball, the trainee is permitted to warm up with the baseball. The young trainees are very surprised to feel the heft of the weight on the arm. At this point they realize the potential harm that could be done by improper delivery or laziness in style and lack of body coordination.

Sketches in the diagram of the epiphysis, better known as the elbow (actually its cartilage), in the Skeletal System show the development of the epiphysis and other cartilage. This area of the arm is crucial to the life of the young pitcher athlete. Care should begin in Little League to provide for the long- term health of the total athlete in which this area of the arm is included.

One reason for the short-lived career of many young pitchers is that most coaches/ parents/instructors are not aware of these developmental stages of the epiphysis. The youngster (boy or girl) is born with very soft connective tissue in the joints of the body. As the child ages, the tissue forms more permanent blood vessels and cartilage which help support the maturing limbs attached above and below. If you, reader, will think: What joint of the body is the least massive (of the major joints), carries the most work of the athlete in ball sports, and has the purpose of movement away from the major mass of muscles supporting it? The epiphysis of the elbow! This joint is the most abused in many sports. Tennis, racquetball, handball, weight training, and most often, baseball pitching.

The development of the epiphysis is a very slow process, and care must be taken to teach the youngster not to throw a curveball. When the youngster prematurely throws the curve, he is aggravating the incompleted development of the supporting tissue and cartilage forming at the elbow (epiphysis) joint. The continued aggravation of this joint will cause pain, and the youngster will not be able to throw. If the child is forced to throw in this condition, permanent "tennis" or "Little League" elbow will result. The child's epiphysis will have calcified and closed off any further development of supporting ligaments and capillaries bringing nutrients to the area. Note the drawings and explanation in the diagram.

Bottom line, do not allow to throw curveballs until the child is fully developed. However, be aware that there are studies which show the standard method of twisting the arm is harmful at any age. Please see the following reports of research studies on harmful curveball when the arm is overrotated. See also the exercises for strengthening the rotator cuff (shoulder muscles) and conditioning the arm for the young pitcher. Figures 6 through 10b (in Chapter 10) show pitches taught at Maitland Sports Training. These pitches have been used without injury to the young athletes' epiphysis or the rotator cuff. They are a good starting point for the young athlete and he (or she in youth leagues) will enjoy a long pitching life. The curveball pitches shown in Figures 2a and 2b are not used with developing athletes unless they are physically mature and developed.

FINGER PRESSURE = BALL MOVEMENT

Notice we use the Point of Concentration Pitching coupled with the safe delivery of the ball by placing the fingers over the threads at desired angles for desired effects. The young pitcher can effectively deliver a "swurve" with the same movement of a curve without the fatal inside twist of the arm. Notice in Figure 2a the 3/4 arm delivery and in Figure 2b the straight over the shoulder delivery.

Figures 2a, 2b, and 2c

Three quarter
Fig. 2b

Over the Top
Fig. 2b

Harmful side arm
Fig. 2c

I feel more power is delivered straight over the shoulder as it is subject to more body momentum than the 3/4 delivery. The 3/4 delivery requires the body to endanger itself by torquing and possibly by forcing the legs to cross over and placing the athlete in a dangerous indefensible position after delivery is completed. Also, the 3/4 delivery can tire the rotator cuff quickly.

Figure 2c shows the side arm, which my pitchers do not use and fielders use only if they are off balance, which I hope, is not frequently. The side arm is another throw dangerous to the rotator cuff as well as to the epiphysis. It places stress on all the wrong sockets at all the angles. The shoulder area can exert enormous pressure on the epiphysis in the whipping motion as well as on the rotator cuff. Remember, there are only so many pitches in an arm, why shorten a baseball pitching career by inducing injury at an early age? See Figure 4a for "submariner" pitch. It is very injurious to the entire arm structure.

I have had coaches (and fathers) stand behind the fence as the youngsters pitched to me in pre-season. One of the parents became upset and accused me of having the athlete throw "junk." I had the athlete show his father how he delivered the ball with finger pressure on the threads and straight over the shoulder without any twist of the arm. The youngster, now in college, still uses this method as a rest between the advanced twisting movements of the arm taught by the college coaches for the curve.

CURVEBALL ARM HARM

Studies have shown that the twisting of the arm may be unnecessary because the action of the arm takes place after the ball has left the hand. It has been demonstrated that placing pressure on the ball at certain angles to the threads and using the threads as a spinoff point affects the spiral and "swurve" of the ball.

I am happy to share evidence presented by Jay Feldman, a contributing author in the October 1984 issue of "American Health" magazine.

In his article, Feldman cites a study done by Phil Swimley, baseball coach at the University of California at Davis, where the path of the curveball was filmed at high speed. His findings have a marked impact on the cessation of many rotator cuff injuries. The article demonstrates the action of the four muscles deep in the shoulder responsible for stabilizing the upper arm bone (humerus) in pitching. These muscles are to hold the humerus in its socket as the arm lifts away from the body. The supraspinatus, infraspinatus, and the teres minor join in a cuff of tendon attached to a ridge on the humeral head. "This cuff is where the injury occurs," says Jay Feldman. I, too, have witnessed many injuries of this type in young pitchers. The throwing of the ball overhead has always been considered an "unnatural" motion. The three tendons are forced against the subacromial arch, a projection of bone that acts as a roof over the shoulder joint. "Current orthopedic theory pinpoints this impingement as a cause of rotator cuff tears," says Jay Feldman.

Mr. Feldman states that "coach Swimley's work offers a significantly new clue to the what and why of rotator cuff injuries. Equally important, it suggests a way of preventing them."

The article also discusses the history of the research done when San Francisco Giants pitcher, Ron Bryant, came to the Davis campus during the off season in 1971 to work on his curveball with Swimley. Ron Bryant went on to win 24 games to lead the league two years after the work with Swimley. With a high speed camera, Swimley filmed Bryant pitching a curve at 3,000 frames per second. The film shows that what coaches have thought happened in the delivery does not occur.

IMAGINED DELIVERY OF CURVEBALL

Coaches have taught that "when the arm reaches the top of its arc, the pitcher gets the ball 'out front' and releases it there, while his arm starts its downward swing. Coaches teach the release of the ball as 'pulling down,' or 'cupping the hand,' since the hand and arm supposedly proceed with a smooth motion into the follow-through."

The article goes on to say that "This delivery is, in fact, a myth!" Swimley stated to Jay Feldman, that "The curve ball motion **feels** like a smooth, continuous one, coming straight down – until you get the slow-motion camera."

Swimley and other professional players did not believe what the film showed. They used other major and minor league players and found the results to be the same.

ACTUAL DELIVERY OF CURVEBALL

(What studies have shown)

As the arm reaches the top of its arc, the pitcher is about to release the ball. Once the arm starts its downward swing, the ball is gone. As in all overhand throwing, the arm continues to rotate from the shoulder until the hand turns completely away from the body. In the most extreme cases, the palm will even turn upward. Because the pitcher has been taught delivery based on an imagined sequence, the pitcher violently reverses the entire momentum of his arm and shoulder. He "de-rotates," twists back, in order to follow through in the "proper" manner.

Swimley continued his interview with Jay Feldman by stating that "because of what they've been taught about how to throw the curve, pitchers wind up fighting the natural rotation of the shoulder in order to try and do something to the ball long after it's been released."

ENGINEERING AND PHYSIOLOGY

Mr. Swimley took his film to a U.C. Davis colleague, Melvin Ramey, a professor of civil engineering and an assistant track coach who works with long jumpers and triple jumpers, reports Jay Feldman.

Ramey stated that "We're treating the human body as a mechanical linkage. In throwing the curve ball, the arm is moving forward at what could be more than 100 miles per hour, and it's fully rotated in one direction. Then, in maybe 3/2000 of a second, the whole thing is rotated 180 degrees the other way." Ramey concludes by saying, "You potentially have relatively large forces and torques existing there."

CHAPTER IV

A NEW DELIVERY: SHORT AND SIMPLE

The next section of the Feldman article deals with a "new delivery" in an attempt to relieve the stress on the shoulder. I, too, became aware of the stress to shoulders of young athletes and have discussed my method of delivering a "safe pitch." I wish to share with my readers the new delivery as researched by Coach Swimley to emphasize the similarity between my observations of thirty years in training and coaching young athletes and the findings of Coach Swimley.

Swimley's "new delivery" emphasizes spinning the ball at the top as you release it (rather than trying to "pull down"), and then letting the arm relax and go where it will without attempting to reverse its natural rotation.

See Figures 3a and 3b.

Figures 3a and Figure 3b

Figure 3a. On top of the ball as per Coach Swimley of U. of C. at Davis, California.

Figure 3b. The de-rotation of the arm as actually happens in curve pitching.

The U. C. Davis coach continued his therapy and showed his film to the American Baseball Coaches Association convention and found that very few coaches were willing to change a one hundred year old method of coaching the curveball.

Swimley helped the then Giants pitcher, Gary Lavelle, after the player had rotator cuff problems. Lavelle stated to Jay Feldman that Swimley went over the importance of strengthening the muscles in the rotator cuff area in order to prolong his career. Lavelle states that he did do the therapy but failed to follow through on the "new delivery." Swimley told Mr. Feldman that he understood Gary Lavelle's hesitancy to "relearn something that got him to the big leagues. But you can start to make a change in college ball or in rookie league."

Nor has everyone yet adopted the "new delivery" and there are still pitches to approach with caution as shown in the following photographs (Figures 4a, 4b, and 4c)

18

Figures 4a, 4b, and 4c.

Figure 4a. The curveball is another pitch causing harm to young athletes.

Figure 4b. Shows the split finger fastball. This pitch has caused harm to professional pitchers, also.

Figure 4c. Submariner pitch.

CHAPTER V

TEACHING SAFE THROWING AT THE ELEMENTARY LEVEL

I would go Coach Swimley's study one level lower and say young athletes should be taught the "natural" arm movement in throwing from Little League age. Otherwise, by the time the youngsters are in high school, they are hooked on the "de-rotation" style which is very hard to retrain. The shoulder injuries are well documented by the second year of high school. Many athletes, as I have already pointed out, are has-beens by their freshman high school years.

I have encountered some parents who had their promising pitchers in "weight lifting" (not weight training) and became disillusioned by the results. The child and parent stop the training with weights because of the increased uncontrollable power in the throw. The trainee blames the weights rather than the method and lack of knowledge by the trainer-coach.

Efforts to inform the trainee of changes in strength and the ability to control the throw with the new strength are paramount in my program (and this book).

The young athlete is taught the changes that will occur as he matures so that he/she is able to cope with new problems and adjustments to his/her athletic performance. The young athlete is coached in both weight training and athletic endeavor so that he/she does not panic when the ball goes out of control the first few times after the first sessions of weight training.

Weight training is a fairly new concept to the elementary through high school student and coaches. The youngsters and their parents are surprised to see the improvements in a short time. The important aspect of any program is the observation of the trainees after training to ensure they learn the skill to master the improved strength. This is an important part of throwing safely with confidence.

Let me repeat a word of warning here about the curveball and its premature use. True, the curveball is a pitch that keeps the batters from too many 300 or 400 seasons. We think of batters who hit the ball three out of ten times as heroes. The curveball is a valuable tool if it does not harm the pitcher. The natural movement of the arm should be learned at a young age. The young athlete can master the movement of the ball by the finger placement on the ball, not by de-rotating the arm after the ball is gone. The young pitchers should learn correct movement on other pitches than the curveball. The curveball should not be attempted until the trainee is fully mature.

CHAPTER VI

THINKING PITCHER – CRUCIAL TO THE GAME

It is important that a manager of a team realize his importance from the Little League up through the minor leagues. Beyond the minor leagues the player will adapt his arm style which will be influenced by the reward of a major league team position. A position on the major league team is guaranteed by the continued good performance of the player. This is the difficulty to which Coach Swimley referred in his attempt to change the style of a major league pitcher. The player is unwilling to change a style that has earned him a living even though the style may be harmful.

The manager of the Little League team can begin at an early age to develop good, safe throwing habits. In order that the young ballplayer be a thinking ballplayer, reasons for the safe throwing should be discussed. It would be beneficial to the child, and his parents, if the physiological basis for the safe throwing method were demonstrated in a pre-season youth league clinic. Youth leagues, we must remember, can include youngsters from ages six to eighteen. The sphere of influence would be dramatic in a good program in youth leagues if all the age levels were consistent in their methodology. The kids would have fun while learning baseball and have the knowledge to pass on to their offspring. I have seen this in effect in my area of influence. The youngsters I trained from age ten in baseball and weight training (for all sports) are now in college or are parents coaching other young ballplayers. I feel as though I have influenced their style with other youngsters and I feel good about it.

This section is to discuss the importance of the mind. The pitcher (and catcher) must be able to think ahead of every pitch. "What will I do if the batter hits a line drive?" thinks our fictitious pitcher. "How did the batter react to the fastball last time at bat?" These questions are constantly on the minds of the pros in the game.

Youth leagues below age thirteen would not need to worry about the style of pitches to be thrown. An immature youngster would do well to throw a fastball and be ready for defense. If the young pitcher has been versed in the total body involvement in throwing without crossing the feet in the delivery, he/she should be ready for the line drive (or at least to get out of the way).

The young pitcher can also learn the techniques of "hiding" the ball as illustrated in Figures 5a, 5b, and 5c. Figure 5a shows the young pitcher "giving away the pitch." Most young pitchers are not able to transfer the ball to the glove while changing the grip before the pitch. To take the best advantage of the batter, it's best to "hide" the ball until the last possible moment as in Figure 5b.

Figure 5c shows the view as though you are the batter. Can you tell what pitch is going to be thrown?" The batter will be surprised since the pitcher has kept the ball hidden until it leaves the glove.

Figures 5a, 5b, and 5c.

Figure 5a. Giving away the pitch (left).

Figure 5b. Hiding the pitch.

Figure 5c. View from the plate.

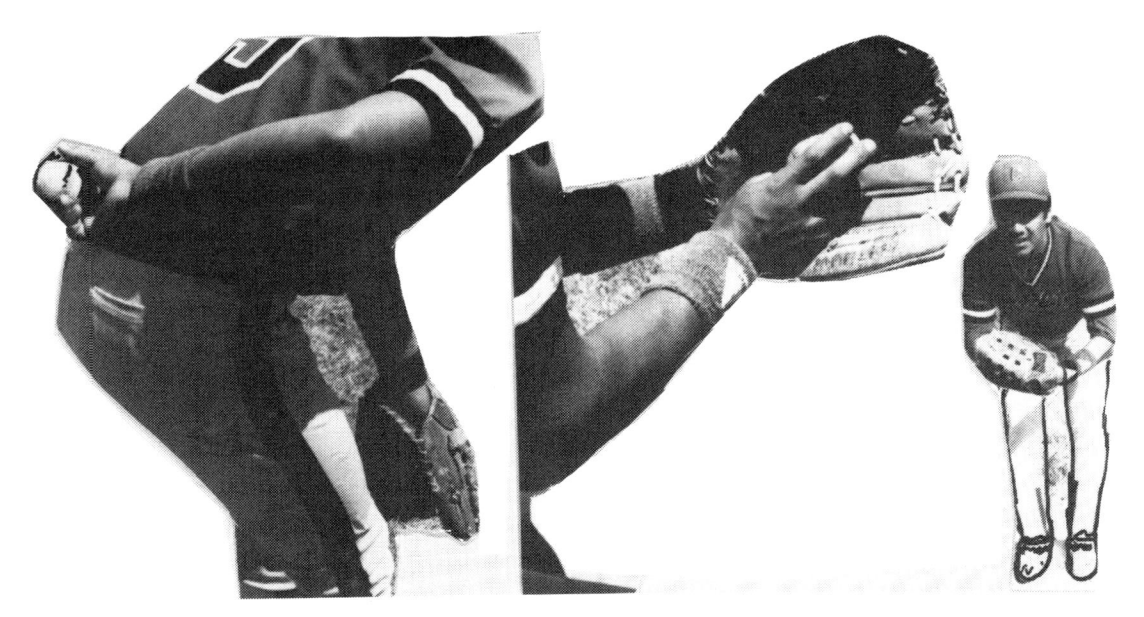

Figure 5a.   Figure 5b.   Figure 5c.

PONY LEAGUES – PLAN PITCHES BEFORE GAMES

The older pitchers in the pony leagues on up through the pro teams should be expected to think in detail of the pitches to be used and the possible defenses if the ball is hit.

Pitchers should be taught a variety of pitches. This will throw the batter off in his timing. In his book, "The Game of Baseball," Gil Hodges states that a manager can do nothing to develop a fastball in a pitcher. The fastball speed comes with the pitcher, says Gil. From the fastball, the curve (safe curve for developed youngsters) is developed. You must have a good fastball if you wish to have an effective "change-up" pitch.

The change-up should be delivered as though it were a fastball in the wind-up. The speed should be off just enough to confuse the batter in his preparation to bring the bat around for the hit. If the ball is too slow the batter will have time to readjust to the slower speed.

I would like to point out that Gil Hodges was referring to a mature ballplayer in the fastball discussion. When you have the opportunity to work with young (eight- to sixteen-year-old) ballplayers, you can demonstrate the total body involvement in the throw. If the youngster matures with the proper training in weights and throwing, and he is of average stature, the fastball should not be a problem. Please remember that not all pitchers pitch for their entire baseball career. Many will not continue in baseball beyond the thirteenth year. Not all pro players play in youth leagues either. Many ballplayers began at age sixteen or seventeen.

I am digressing. The final statement I wish to make for the subject of the thinking pitcher is that if the pitcher fails to control his emotions during the game he will not be an effective leader in the games. The other team members will feel they have been abandoned and that the pitcher has resolved that he will not help the team win.

TEACHING MIND CONTROL

I have seen many young pitchers lose their cool in a game. They are permitted to exhibit this behavior from age ten to pony league. They are never counseled as to methods of relaxation or the acceptance that a batter will hit the ball occasionally.

Pitchers need to be taught that baseball is a game of averages. If a hitter is due for a hit and the pitcher happens to be pitching the right pitch, the ball will be hit. The manager can attempt to teach the youngster the best areas for the ball to enter the strike zone. Certain areas of the strike zone are prone to strikes while others may lead to a high foul ball pop out.

On one of my teams in Little League, the youngsters were aged ten through twelve years. Some of the players were ready to turn thirteen and were very mature, large youngsters. One such youngster came to the plate and you could see the mass deflation and resignation of my total team in the field.

I called upon a rather stocky, aggressive lad (from right field) to pitch to this batter. You could see the ten-year-old's grin as he ran in from right field. We had been praticing one pitch for this batter.

The younger pitcher had been instructed to pitch to the large batter (right-handed) inside and just below the elbow. The batter liked to crowd the plate. This pitch forced him back, and he attempted to back off the ball and hit it. This jammed him up and forced him to hit the ball just above the grip and he popped straight up to the pitcher. The large boy was surprised and the pitcher was elated as were the spectators. Bottom line . . . every pitch does not have to be a strike. Help the pitcher think; to use the batter's weaknesses.

CHAPTER VII

CATCHER FOR THE DEFENSE

A catcher is one of the best allies a pitcher has on the team. Gil Hodges states that catchers in youth league clubs can be taught to help the pitcher through bad calls by the umpire. In his book, "How to Coach, Manage and Play Little League Baseball," Charles Einstein, former coach and president of Little League, says the catcher is perhaps the best athlete on the team. The catcher can be used for pitching also at this level of play. The ideal situation, according to Mr. Einstein, would be the coach developing a good catcher before worrying about the pitching.

If the team has two good pitchers and one good catcher it is blessed in Little League. This will remove the need for any of the pitchers to catch.

Getting back to the catcher as being the best ally to the pitcher in bad umpiring, Mr. Einstein explains several ways the catcher can assist the pitcher. The catcher should be as close to the hitter as possible. This position closes the distance between the hitter and the catcher. Since many Little League umpires call the ball in the catcher's glove rather than where it crosses the plate, the distance needs to be shortened. The catcher can "bring in" every close pitch. The glove will be brought to the strike zone where the umpire has been calling them in the catcher's glove. The catcher cannot exercise too much bravado in this "adjusting" the ball. He can only "adjust the close ones. The pitcher should be well versed in the fastball. The less dip the ball has, the greater chance for call strikes. Many umpires call the ball where it dips to the catcher's glove rather than where it crosses over the plate in the strike zone."

Mr. Einstein further states that most Little Leaguers cannot hit a fastball, and this pitch should be the only one thrown in the younger age groups. The older boys should be taught the proper method for the curveball if they are physically mature and do not throw sidearm. The curveball is to be thrown straight over the shoulder or at a "three quarter arm." No Little League should experiment with the "screwball" and definitely should not throw this pitch. It causes great strain on the rotator cuff and the epiphysis.

Managers should not expect young Little League players to remember a lot of strategy. Defensive strategies should be short and simple. This includes the pitcher covering most infield positions, and not confusing the second baseman about the pitcher's area of responsibility and the shortstop's areas.

CHAPTER VIII

LACK OF FIELD TIME IN LITTLE LEAGUE?

Gil Hodges, too, feels that Little League teams do not allow the kids to play enough. Part of the reason is that parents and other adults do not always have the time to spend with the kids. It is a shame that the kids must depend on the adults to play ball. I point this out in Chapter XIII when I quote the remarks in the same vein made by Whitey Herzog, manager of the St. Louis Cardinals.

In this light I would like to mention the practice of many high school coaches to not allow the pitchers to bat. I think this is a big mistake. The young players are scouted, and hitting is an important part of playing ball.

The coaches who prevent the pitchers from hitting are being very selfish. They are not allowing the youth to show his ability as a total ballplayer. Many high school pitchers will not pitch as life goes on; why not let them enjoy the game? Hitting the ball is the best part of the game. Also, if a scout sees a potential shortstop — or other infield position — in your pitcher, the lad will not have the opportunity to show his "bat" to the scout.

Gil Hodges says also that the youth leaguer should be trained to play "Little League" baseball. You cannot use the same coaching techniques as you would on a regulation field. The fences are played differently as well as the infield distances.

Gil Hodges quotes Willie Mays when asked to comment on the theory of playing baseball. Willie Mays said, "When somebody throws the ball, I hit it. When somebody hits it, I catch it."

CHAPTER IX

MAKE IT HARD TO HIT

In youth baseball the circumference and weight of the ball varies according to the age level of the league. At the youngest age levels the child need only be concerned with the speed of the ball. As the child matures and develops power and strength (with the help of this weight training program) the youth will need to develop a talent for causing the ball to move deceptively toward the batter.

Tom Seaver in his excellent book, "The Art of Pitching," describes various changes a pitcher goes through as he gets higher "on the ladder of pro baseball." The higher he gets, the more he is taken advantage of by the batters. This observation can well be taken by the aspiring high school and college pitchers. The "Arizona Republic" newspaper in 1982 carried an article listing circumstances of young pitchers who had been worked too hard and had to enter therapy if they were drafted by a pro team.

This book is about prevention of such atrocities. The prevention begins at the T-Ball level and continues throughout the developmental life of the athlete. After the athlete matures, he must engage in training to maintain the gains in conditioning and strength earned in the developmental stages of youth.

If a pitcher hits a slump, he should be taught to throw low strikes. The pitcher should not panic and "go wild" or become emotionally upset. Tom Seaver says, as had Gil Hodges, that a pitcher who loses his head is not good for himself or the team.

Throwing low strikes permits the batter to see only the top of the ball as it comes about six inches above the knee. I like my pitchers to throw low and inside if they are in a slump. This allows for a better chance of a ball being hit by the skinny part of the bat.

The pitcher must not allow the batter to hit the ball with the meat of the bat. The meat of the bat is about eight inches long and two and three quarters thick. If the pitcher can prevent contact with that part of the bat, he will enjoy a good game.

Tom Seaver's book deals with the more mature aspiring pitcher. His points should be considered for the younger athlete aspiring to high school and college ball, and, perhaps, beyond. Know your mistakes. If you made a bad pitch and got away with it, remember it so an alert batter will not get a chance at another mistake.

PROBLEMS AND TACTICS

Always try to get the first batter. It seems to have a negative effect on the next batters and boosts the morale of the defense. To get the first batter out you must stay ahead of the batter on the ball-strike count. A count of 0-2 or 1-2 causes the batter some anxiety which can assist the pitcher in making the out.

Remember to hide the ball from the batter and any base coaches or base runners. The element of surprise is lost if, in high school ball and up, the batter is tipped off as to the pitch coming at him. Review Figures 5a, 5b, and 5c.

Pitching from the stretch involves the same principles as pitching from the full wind-up. The difference being the angle of the pivot foot to the rubber. In the stretch pitch, your foot is parallel to the rubber. In the full wind-up, the foot is placed on the rubber with the toe facing the batter ready for a pivot on the wind-up. No matter what type of pitch, do not overthrow or allow the arm to cross the body which can cause severe injury to the arm and shoulder.

To have a long pitching career you must coordinate your legs and arms. Be sure to land with your lead foot under your lead arm and the pivot foot under your throwing arm. When I have seen kids having a problem crossing over their body I would place a bat or glove in the path of the offending foot. The pitcher would become conscious of the object and bring his pivot foot first left of an imaginary line. I have used a rope at times to get the trainee used to the placement of the foot. I would raise the rope as the foot was being placed down on the throw and gently nudge the foot if it crossed over center. This is something I learned from training race horses. We would gently nudge the jumping horses' hind hooves if they came too close to the top rail of the jump.

DRILL FOR BODY COORDINATION IN THROWING

Coordination involves the entire body. The weight training program in this book will assist in the development of the throwing arm as well as the non-throwing arm. Tom Seaver discusses a "lazy glove arm" in "The Art of Pitching." He recommends a drill where the player drops to his knees in the outfield and throws the ball to another player about thirty feet away. As the trainee improves the throw from the knees, he should slowly back up until about forty feet from his partner, says Mr. Seaver. This drill will develop the proper 45 degree angle with the left arm and knee since the player can't use the lower body. After a relaxed drill in the outfield, the pitcher should be ready for the mound again.

Remember, younger players should not be overtrained in any drill. Teach the fundamentals before engaging in any drills requiring unusual strain. I would recommend that Tom Seaver's drill be reserved for mature high school trainees.

CHAPTER X

MOST IMPORTANT PITCH

Remember, the fastball is the most important pitch in baseball. Everything else is off the fastball pitch. To confuse the batter you must be able to change the speed of the ball. The change-up pitch is one that will catch a batter off guard if it is thrown in the same manner as the fastball. Any change in the wind-up or body torque will tip off the batter and give him time to readjust his swing of the bat or his stance. Throwing an inside fastball reminds the batter that you are in control of the plate. The inside pitch forces the batter back, ideally preventing him from reaching the outside corner pitch.

The youngster may have days where his fastballs actually accelerate during the game. Nolan Ryan has days when his fastball goes from 90 miles an hour to 100 miles an hour, says Tom Seaver. Can you imagine the surprise of the batters on those days. Reggie Jackson says in his book, "Inside Hitting," that he was never embarrassed to be struck out by Nolan Ryan because Ryan was a very effective pitcher.

FASTBALL GRIPS

Every human hand is different and will hold the ball where it feels most comfortable. I teach my trainees to throw the fastball with the fingers and thumb across the wide part of the threads. As mentioned elsewhere, this causes a spin which makes the ball appear smaller as it approaches the batter. The size of the child will determine where the ball feels most comfortable. Experiment with the grip.

The pressure points should also be experimental. The trainee should picture the action he wants the ball to take and try pressuring with each finger until he realizes the speed he wants. Sometimes this will be the index finger (next to the thumb), then try with the pressure on the middle finger.

Try the pressure with thumb and then without pressure on the thumb. Try the throw with the thumb across the bottom threads and then without the thumb across the seam (threads).

Pictured in Figures 6, 7, and 8 are some grips suggested for the rising fastball which behaves according to the backward spin placed on the ball in the pitch. I will not discuss the Bernoulli's Law which deals with gases interacting with velocity and gravity to overcome the downward motion, causing the ball to rise. The reader may wish to research this phenomenon if interested.

The pictures used in this book are of the students who trained at Maitland Sports Training. They are not photographs of the hands of the professional ballplayers. The students are shown duplicating or following the techniques of the professional ballplayers named.

Figure 6

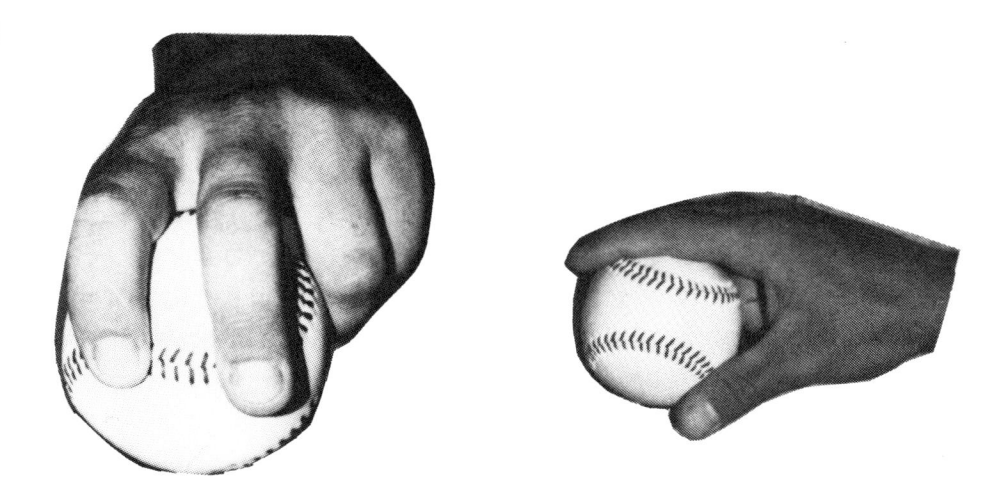

Figure 6. Rising Fastball...as used by Nolan Ryan.

Note that youngsters may be unable to reach the spread of the fingers as shown in Figure 6. The child should be permitted to find his or her point of comfort. I favor this grip because it really puts a good spin on the ball.

Steve Carlton holds his fingers closer together but holds the ball farther out on the tips of his fingers. The tip of the thumb is across the bottom seam. Please experiment with this grip. There are many others that differ only in spacing of fingers and pressure points. The two discussed here are good starting points for experimentation.

Get to know the release point for the rising fastball. You will release the ball at the ten o'clock position. You may feel the hand is releasing at the twelve o'clock position. However, because of the position of the release from behind your ear and the exaggerated arch of the arm it will release at the ten o'clock position. The wrist should be relaxed not stiff. Snap your wrist at the release with force and determination. Keep your fingers on top of the ball and drive toward the plate. A slight turning of the wrist inward or outward will cause the ball to react differently. The batter will be kept off guard because the rising fastball will develop a slight unpredictable movement.

Young pitchers should be cautioned that the wrist movement is slight. We do not want to encourage young undeveloped athletes to use the curveball at this point.

The younger the pitcher, the more the straight fastballs are thrown with no deviation.

THE SINKING FASTBALL

The sinking fastball is made to feel heavier upon reaching the catcher. As I mentioned earlier, a tired pitcher would do well to throw the ball low. The sinking fastball has that property which causes the batter to hit the top of the ball and to ground out. The right-hander may be forced to hit the ball with the skinny part of the bat while the left-hander would be forced to hit the ball off the end of his bat from a right-handed pitcher.

My trainees are taught the grip used by Tom Seaver. They have found it most effective because the seams offer a good point of identification as they take the ball out of the glove for the pitch. They also state they feel more control on the sinker using the fingers and the thumb on the seams. The thumb crosses the seam on the underside. Note the picture in Figure 7 shows the fingers placed on the pads along the narrow seams. The inside of the thumb rests on the seam underneath the ball.

Pressure may be applied by the index finger which causes the ball to sink so that the batter's chances of hitting a ground out are almost assured. You may wish to try to vary the index finger and the middle finger to keep the batter guessing.

Figure 7. Sinking Fastball

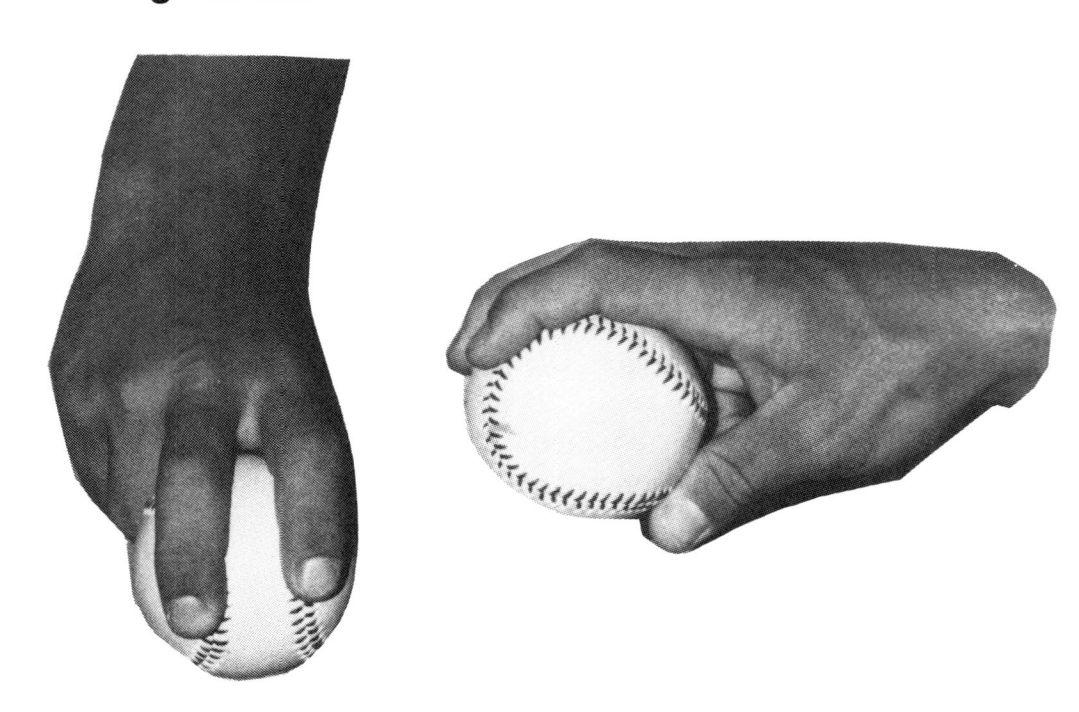

The sinker does not spin as fast as the rise because you are not using as many threads as with the rising fastball.

Variations of these fastballs can be accomplished by placing the fingers at different angles across the seams. The "swurve" I discussed at the beginning of the book is such a variation. Again I say, experiment.

VARIATIONS OF THE CHANGE-UP PITCH

Figure 8. Change-up

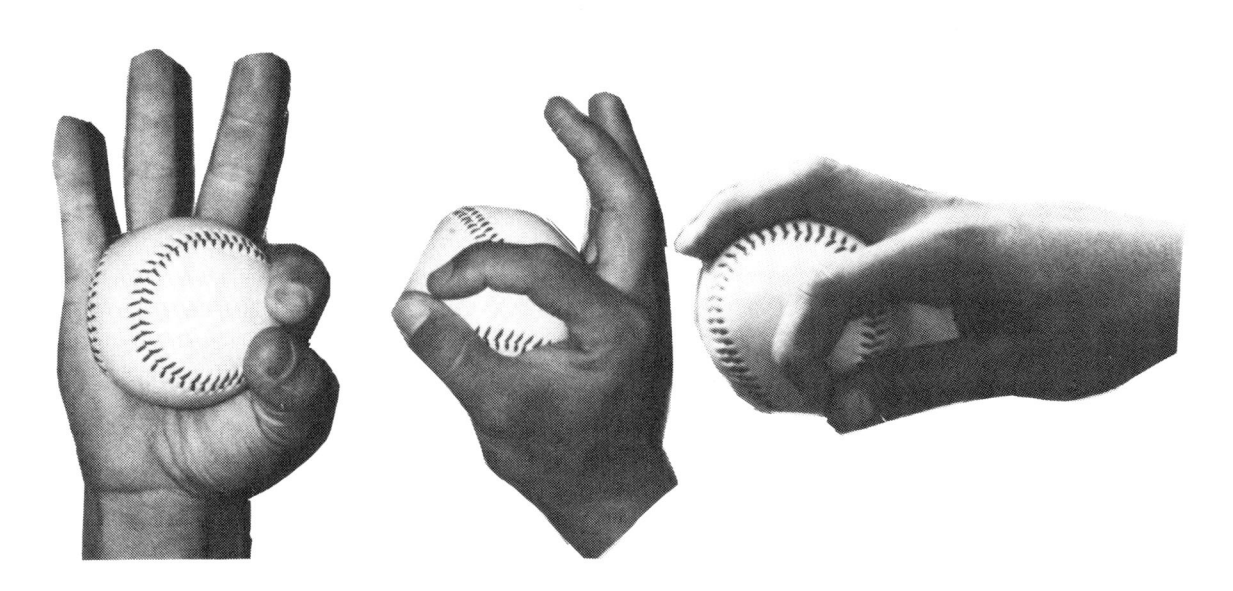

Figure 8.   Change-up Pitch   Three Views

The change-up offers the change in speed pitch that will confuse the batter. It must be thrown as though it were a fastball. The pictures are self-explanatory: Notice the power finger is removed from the ball and placed on the side (index finger). Practice—practice, innovate—innovate, throw—throw—throw.

CHAPTER XI

PITCHES FOR THE ADVANCED TRAINEE

THE CURVEBALL

When I began to write this book I had in mind to discuss the beginning ballplayer and then write a separate work for the high school or college level pitcher. I rethought my efforts and felt that this work should incorporate the full development of the athlete through his adult years. Thus, the coach or parent will have all the necessary information to carry the child from T-Ball to college ball. My confidence in the adults overseeing the young trainees using this book is that they will be able to prevent the undeveloped young trainee from using this portion of the book until he or she is mature and has reached the potential for his body (especially arm) development. No beginning ballplayer should employ any methods in this chapter until fully mature, muscle development has occurred, and there is no evidence of injury to the arm from past performance on the field.

The curveball and slider are the most demanding pitches on the arm of a professional athlete. I have seen irreparable damage done to Little Leaguers because of overzealous coaches and parents in allowing the child to throw curves. Figures 9a and 9b show the curveball grips used by Nolan Ryan and Tom

Seaver. As mentioned in the last chapter the pictures used in this book are of my trainees, not of the hands of the professional ballplayers.

Figures 9a and 9b

Figure 9a. Nolan Ryans Curve Ball Grip

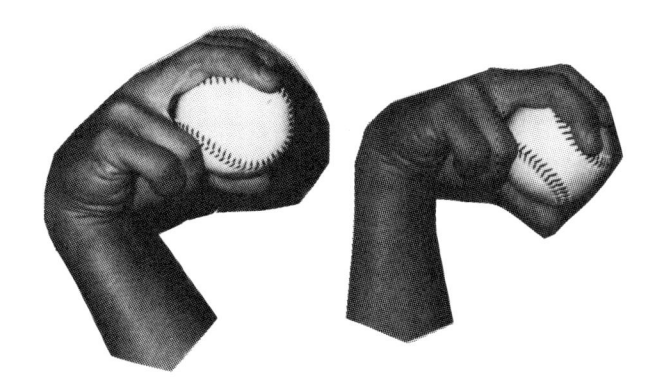

Figure 9b. Tom Seavers Curve Ball Grip

Note that Nolan Ryan grips his curveball across the wide seams. His grip is more off center than his fastball and farther back in his hand. Nolan's thumb pad is in firm contact with the bottom seam. Mr. Ryan applies heavy pressure to the bottom of the ball in the throw.

Nolan Ryan does not bend his wrist on the curveball. He uses a straight and relaxed wrist. I taught my trainees this method before I learned that Nolan Ryan used this style. It seems to make sense that less harm to the arm would result if the wrist was not forced to a more unnatural movement.

Notice the difference in the grip used by Tom Seaver compared to Nolan Ryan's. Tom Seaver states that he could not pitch with the straight wrist as can Nolan Ryan. Again I say to the mature athlete, experiment; see which grip gives you the best control.

The curveball is not a speed pitch. It is a pitch to be used to confuse the batter by its change in speed and direction as close to the batter as possible. If a curve breaks too far from the plate, the batter will have time to readjust his stance and check his swing.

Mature pitchers should study the behavior of the ball as it crosses the plate. Try different pressure points with index finger or middle finger. Try different positions of the ball far back in the hand as Nolan Ryan, or farther out as Tom Seaver.

THE SLIDER

The slider is another method to confuse the batter. It breaks down slightly as it crosses the plate. It does not break as much as the curveball, but it confuses the batter because it breaks so near the strike zone. Pitchers who have practiced the slider can be very deceptive in causing the batter to think a fastball is coming right over the plate. When the ball falls low and outside (or inside) the batter does not have time to adjust.

Tom Seaver says more home runs are hit on bad sliders than on any other pitch. If the pitch is allowed to "hang," it will be hit. Keep your finger on top of the ball, not the sides, and you will avoid the "flat" slider.

Many people do not realize how much damage an improperly thrown curveball can do to an arm. The slider can do even more harm than the regular curveball. Tom Seaver states that the Los Angeles Dodgers do not permit their minor league pitchers to throw the slider at all. Young pitchers should not be coached in the slider until fully mature and full muscular development has occurred. The young pitcher should be introduced to the curveball before considering a slider after maturity is completed. If he can't control a curveball, he should not throw a slider. Tom Seaver says Nolan Ryan never throws a slider.

The slider is properly thrown by a slight pulling down with the elbow at the last moment. This causes the ball to move laterally in the hitting zone. Tom Seaver compares the movement to throwing a knife as in mumblety-peg. Some say it's like throwing a football where the elbow takes all the pressure in the throw.

Figures 10a and 10b

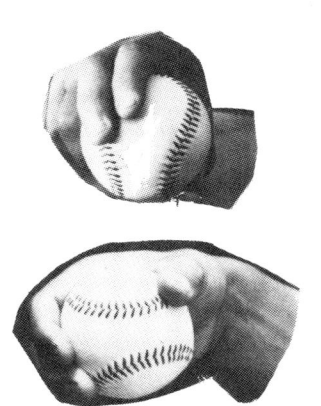

Figure 10a. Slider Grip
used by Gil Hodges
(Top and bottom)

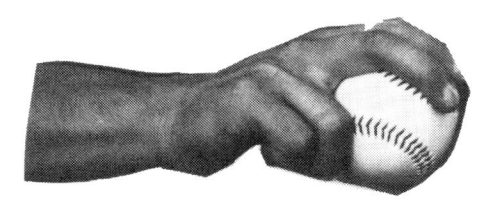

Figure 10b Slider Grip
used by Steve Carlton
(Top and side view)

Notice the grip in Figure 10a. The slider is held farther back in the hand though it appears to be similar to the rising fastball. This will deceive the batter into thinking he will be getting a fastball pitch. The placement of the fingers inside the long seam with the thumb along a narrow seam underneath causes the ball to rotate as a fastball, but to change altitude as it approaches the plate.

In Figure 10b we see the slider as thrown by Steve Carlton. He uses the same grip as with his curveball. He grips the two wide seams across the smaller gap with his thumb on top of the seam under the ball. The ball is held farther out on the finger tips. He uses equal pressure on the index finger and middle finger which are almost a quarter inch apart. More pressure is applied with his thumb.

Steve Carlton throws his slider from the 2:30 or 2:45 o'clock angle. His curveball is thrown from the 12:00 o'clock angle over the top.

CHAPTER XII

RELIEF PITCHERS AND THEIR PITCHES

The demands of throwing a couple of hundred pitches a day can tax the best arms. We must remember to count the warm ups the pitcher throws prior to taking the mound. One way the pitcher's arm is salvaged is by the introduction of the relief pitcher.

Coit Wilhelm was the first relief pitcher used in the 1940s and 1950s. This practice has proven to increase the life of the starting pitcher. Joe Black was the first black relief pitcher to win a World Series in 1952. Joe Black won fifteen games and saved fifteen games that year with the Brooklyn Dodgers.

SPLIT FINGER FASTBALL

Elroy Face used his split finger fastball when relieving for the Pittsburgh Pirates. Elroy's career was remarkable in that he was not a tall, long-armed player as we visualize the powerful throwers of today. Elroy had a 19 and 1 in his career which lasted from the '40s into the '60s. This man was about five feet nine inches tall and was all business on the mound. He was one of the first, if not the first, to use the split finger fastball in the major leagues. He used many other pitches during the course of a game which, no doubt, contributed to his long life on the mound.

Many modern day major league teams are experiencing problems with the health of their pitching staff because of the use of the split finger fastball. This pitch (See Figure 11a.) is not for everyone. Even the professionals are learning they must have enormous hands to use this pitch. The aspiring amateurs would be well advised not to use this pitch. It can shorten your pitching career before it begins. It has already ended some aspiring professional pitchers' careers.

The importance of the relief pitcher can be witnessed by the baseball fan today. Phil and Joe Niekro and Lou Gosage showed the style of pitches used to deceive the batter today — Lou Gosage with his "submariner." Recall the submariner illustrated in Figure 4c. Do you think you could pitch that ball as a student game after game? I don't think so.

Figures 11a and 11b

Figure 11a. A Split Finger Fastball

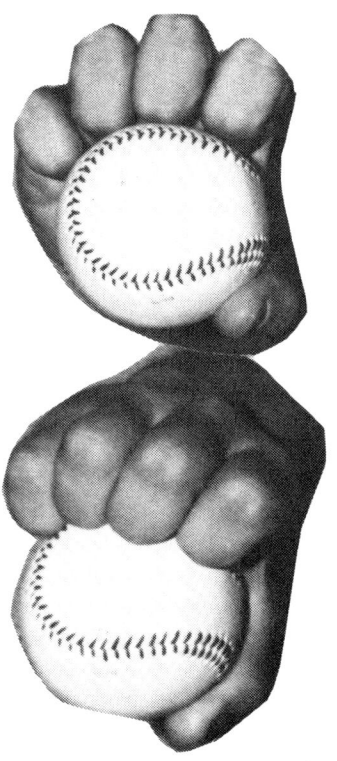

Figure 11b. Knuckleball

THE KNUCKLEBALL

The father-son relievers, Phil and Joe Niekro, threw a knuckleball that was very effective. Phil's manner of throwing prolonged his career and has kept his arm healthy well into his forties.

Note in Figure 11b how the knuckleball is held. The young pitcher must have good sized hands for the knuckleball as well as for the split finger fastball. I say again, develop the fastball and as you mature you may want to try some of these "junk" pitches.

IMPORTANCE OF THE CHANGE-UP

It is important that the young, strong pitcher realize the importance of a change-up pitch. He should not be so invested in muscling the ball that he fails to see the value in a change of speed ball that keeps the batter off balance. The basic change-up pitches as described in Figure 8 should be mastered by the young pitcher before any "junk" pitches are attempted.

I feel I must keep reminding the reader that this book is written to prolong the active life of the ballplayer (or any athlete) from age eight to adulthood. The practices for training the arm can be for any sport requiring arm strength: racquetball, tennis, golf, swimming, and many others.

I have met many ballplayers who never made the college or pro leagues and expressed their anguish that no one ever took the time to teach them the proper training methods when they were young. They felt used by coaches and trainers who never took the time to teach them why throwing curveballs and sliders before maturity was a bad idea. Many uninformed coaches in high school overuse the pitchers and do not allow them proper rest between games. By the time the youngster is an adult interested in trying out for the pros (and in most cases, just trying out for high school ball from Little League) they find their arm has no strength for throwing.

CHAPTER XIII

RESTING THE TOTAL ATHLETE

I've heard Little League rules discussed among the coaches stating the rule for how much rest the child's arm needed after a six-inning game. They talked as though the appendage (arm) was a separate entity that the young pitcher had rented out to them. Many coaches and parents seem to put unnecessary emotional stress on the child by expecting the athlete to perform a set number of innings so they can plan their strategy for the rest of the week's games. They (the parents/coaches) are terribly upset if the child athlete is unable to complete the pre-set game because of a sore arm or deflated ego. Many coaches will force the child to throw until the child begins to cry, further embarrassing the young athlete.

The parents become upset if their child is not played, and the coach becomes upset because now he must use his "star" pitcher for the "easy" game which will cut down the chances of the "important" game later in the week. The child who could not finish his innings may have been subjected to six pitches per batter not counting foul balls. This would be at least 50 to 60 pitches not counting foul balls and the acumen of his fielders. For a young player to play just three innings under these conditions would tax the total athlete. If the coaches and parents could understand the total muscle body commitment to throwing the ball across the plate, they would have more empathy for the young athlete.

BODY FATIGUE IN PITCHING

The adults think of the child's arm as being "tired." The coaches do not understand that "tired" is systemic and lactic acid is the waste product of working muscle and can affect the entire muscle structure of the body. The arm may hurt, but the body became less able to absorb the torque of the throw, and the arm was forced to absorb the full brunt of the delivery . . . in the rotator cuff and the epiphysis if throwing curveballs or not following through on "safe" pitches.

It will do no good to prescribe the amount of rest a young athlete should have between innings pitched, as each inning can be 30 to 100 pitches. The factor must be the total condition of the athlete and his ability to recover from the last work day. I would definitely say that a young athlete should not pitch for at least a week if his arm hurt after the last day worked. The coaches should not pressure the child by benching him during this period of recovery. He should be allowed to play in a position that will least tax his arm, and the child should be counseled as to the reason for this.

I believe no child should be pitched more than 150 pitches per game. That figure considers three innings of seven pitches to five batters. The pitcher would cease to be the hero of the team and the team would learn to function as a team rather than relying on the "arm." It would also force many youth league baseball coaches to "coach and train" rather than "recruit" the young athletes even at age ten.

ORGANIZED YOUTH BASEBALL CAN PREVENT EXPERIENCE

Whitey Herzog, well known baseball player of the past and known as an outstanding manager for the St. Louis Cardinals, voiced his opinion on the Today Show on March 25, 1985.

Mr. Herzog was asked what he thought of the various youth baseball leagues today. He stated that the children failed to learn to hit or catch if they were the smaller kids on the team. He went on to say that the trend in these leagues is to put the biggest kid on the mound to pitch to the smaller kids who never get a chance to hit.

Since the batters never get a crack at the ball, the fielders never learn to field the ball. Mr. Herzog went on to say that when he was a youngster, they "played sandlot ball from sunup to sundown. There were no umpires or parents to make rules or show disappointment if you errored or struck out. It did not make any difference if you had enough players or too many players, everybody played."

I agree with Mr. Herzog's observations in that the present leagues seem to be fashioned after the major leagues in expectations of the young athlete. The children are pressured to perform beyond the capabilities of their growing bodies. This is especially true of pitchers. Too much emphasis is placed on the acumen of the pitcher and not enough on fielding.

As the child becomes more mature physically and emotionally, he would be expected to use the skills learned more adroitly. This adeptness would follow naturally if the child were "coached" correctly and given the skills training at an early age. Of course not every child cares to go on to high school ball and finds other sports more suited to her or him. The parents and coaches must be supportive of the child's choices as long as they are not harmful.

Whitey Ford stated on his book tour that he would have his child play a field position until well into his teens because the continued pitching limits the throws in the arm.

There are many ballplayers who threw curveballs from age twelve and are now unable to throw the ball from the outfield because of overuse of the arm at a young age.

AFTERWORD TO PITCHING SECTION

I hope my readers enjoy their training while having a good time playing baseball. I enjoy training most of the kids in my program. There are always the few who seem disinterested in certain aspects of the training regimen. I have difficulty in getting some of the kids to do the stretches before weight training or throwing the ball. These are important areas to consider when training youngsters. They want to do everything at once or do it their own way. The trainer/instructor must convey a sense of humor toward the young trainees while controlling the program.

I am extremely proud of the youngsters, both boys and girls, who have been through my program in Phoenix, Arizona. Even though many have not gone on to college or pro ball, many have found better leagues or other semi-pro leagues and still play. Some are playing college ball and hope to be considered for a professional team. One boy attended college and during the summer break, he teaches younger boys hockey at a local rink. This youngster has been in my program since age eleven and he still comes over for a refresher in training when he gets a chance.

This young man, Victor Solis, Jr., has been an excellent hockey and baseball player. He chose to give up playing hockey regularly after he graduated from high school. He received a college scholarship for baseball. He graduated and is pursuing a master's degree in sports physiology and training.

Victor gave up regular hockey so he could continue playing baseball year 'round. It was a tough choice. He still plays hockey at least once a week with local teams of adults, some of whom were professional hockey players.

A summer job is another factor that limits Victor's time. He is an amazing young man who still finds time to stay fit and help others. He has always been an excellent student as well as an excellent athlete. It is to Victor Solis, Jr., and all the boys and girls like him that I dedicate this book.

This book is also dedicated to the parents of youngsters who give the time and effort to make themselves available to the wholesome activities in sports and training.

CHAPTER XIV

MUSCULAR DEVELOPMENT AND EMOTIONAL READINESS FOR COMPETITION

The body needs structure and protection in the areas housing the vital organs. The body receives its structure from the skeleton which also protects the vital organs. Connective tissues develop into cartilage and then bone. Some "bones" are cartilage at birth and do not develop into bone until about age 25. The epiphysis of the elbow would be a prime example of this slow developing area. I keep referring to this most important area of the arm because a pitcher cannot pitch unless the elbow is in good condition.

An infant's bones number 330. The adult undergoes a skeletal change which fuses bones together making a total of 206. The limbs become longer and the chest widens as maturity approaches. See the diagrams following Chapter I.

To the pitcher, the most important joint is the elbow, which is a hinge joint. The elbow receives lubricating fluid from a membrane which lines the joint capsule. Each bone end has a layer of cartilage. This is also true for the ball and socket joint of the shoulder. This shoulder joint (actually its muscles) is usually referred to as the rotator cuff, another important joint for the pitcher.

PROFILE OF DEVELOPMENT - AGE SEVEN

The seven-year-old begins minute eye-hand coordination tasks such as coloring, drawing, clay modeling, etc. He reads and watches television. He is content to "watch" rather than "do." At times he/she can be very adept at learning and at other times he/she can be very forgetful. He will be in "over this head" at times and become frustrated with a task he has started. I have seen many seven-year-olds give up on building plastic models that have been too sophisticated for the child.

This child can hop on one foot for six feet and jump about two feet from a platform. The seven-year-old develops friendships at school, sometimes a special friend. He/she is beginning to take pride in hygiene and physical appearance. He is too young emotionally to interact in team sports. Physically he/she has started to develop coordination for simple tasks of play and climbing.

PROFILE OF DEVELOPMENT - AGE EIGHT

The eight-year-old develops an acute interest in what's going on around him (and others). He/she forms new relationships and is aware of other people's opinions and concerns. He can now describe events and objects and appreciates the peculiarities of activities. The child remains on a plateau until his teens. He is more independent of adults and has visions of his future as a person. The brain is not fully developed at this point, and the child will not attain sexual maturity or adult stature for many years.

The eight-year-old boy or girl can be introduced to team sports with the emphasis placed on fun and fitness. Soccer is an excellent team sport for this age thanks to the number of players on each team and the consistent activity on the field. If the child becomes winded in soccer, he can walk and rest, there will be someone to fill in for him with no hard feelings.

The eight-year-old interested in baseball can join a T-Ball league team and begin the rudiments of hitting the ball and running the bases. This also should be done in the spirit of fun.

CONTINUUM OF SOCIALIZATION

There is a continuum of socialization that begins at age five and continues to age twelve. This is when the child is learning the "rules" of making and keeping friends. It is at this age that the child would be vulnerable to an insensitive coach/instructor who demanded too much from the developing child emotionally and physically. I know many teenagers who had the potential to become great footballers, track runners, and baseball players who were turned off to sports completely because of an overbearing, insensitive coach or instructor.

Such insensitive instructors and coaches spurred me to write my first book, "Beginning Weight Training For Young Athletes." I wrote that book in an attempt to stop the coaches of a junior high school from making the students do aerobics and sit-ups on a cement basketball court. When the instructors were requested to cease this practice, some became very angry and felt the child needed pain to get stronger. Eventually the practice did stop and the kids were permitted to use mats or go to the grassy area. I donated copies of my book to that school and other junior high schools in town.

PUBERTY AND THE CHANGE

The girl's pelvis widens and more fat appears on the hips. Menstruation can begin at age twelve but usually will occur between ages fourteen to seventeen. Each person has his/her own biological clock, and no alarm should be felt if the child's development takes longer than that of others her/his age. The skeletal growth stops around age seventeen or eighteen. The girl's breast continues to develop, and there is weight gain into the early twenties.

The boys experience a rapid growth in height at puberty. The shoulders broaden, the voice deepens, and hair thickens over the entire body. The boys have a sudden gain in strength, and height and weight continue to increase into the early twenties.

PERSONAL OBSERVATIONS

I have trained and coached boys and girls together from first grade through the ninth grade. I have found that girls who were given a chance to engage in sports with boys and treated equally with the same expectations were capable of competing at the same level of dexterity and skill until well into puberty. After the girls reached puberty they parted to compete with their own gender. They still enjoyed sports but were not capable of competing with the boys because of the change of muscle strength and body structure.

The boys enjoy a surge of muscle maturity and strength as well as a gain in height and weight. The girl's upper body strength is about 16 percent less than that of the adolescent male. This requires that girls engage in sports more suited to their abilities and strengths as they mature. They certainly cannot engage in football with boys because of the difference in upper body strength. I know there are exceptions to this rule and I laud the girls who compete with the boys in high school. However, they are the exception. I am happy to see that the boys accept the girls on the playing field if they have the talent and are aware of the risk involved.

CONCLUSION OF DEVELOPMENT CHAPTER

To end this chapter on development I feel compelled to state again that every child is different. They all develop at their own pace. In the chapters that follow I will offer a weight training program and other forms of exercise especially for the pitcher. Other positions may use the same training methods to enhance their batting and throwing.

The age of the child in training matters only in the amount of supervision available. I would not permit a young Little League age child to perform the same training methods as the adolescent unless they were both of the same strength and needed the careful structure and supervision of the beginner.

No snapping or sudden jerks of any joint area should be done by any athlete. All movements are to be deliberate and done carefully.

CAUTIONS AND RECOMMENDATIONS

I would not insist that a child below age twelve enter into a weight training program regularly as their interests change quickly. The program for the Little League child should be short but effective and fun. Supervision available and knowledge of the trainer are the only factors which determine the age a child should be in weight training. The National Strength and Conditioning Association has done a study in this area. Request a copy from the Association.

Please remember that the repetitions and sets of exercises described in this book are for generally healthy and somewhat experienced youngsters. If any youngster shows signs of strain or fatiguing at intervals other than listed in this workout, the set and repetition should be altered to fit the strength and condition of the young athlete. That is, if a schedule calls for three sets of ten repetitions, and the youngster shows straining and muscle fatigue at his/her second set at the fifth repetition, the youngster should be permitted to work at that level until the strength and endurance are built up. Sometimes the youngster will have to mature physically while attaining the added strength and endurance. There is a curve of "natural strength," which must coincide with "acquired strength" in the younger and immature athlete.

CHAPTER XV

STRETCHES

There are several stretches which my trainees do to loosen and relax muscles before the onset of weight training or pitching. Stretching the arm is no more crucial than stretching the legs and torso of the pitcher. The pitcher uses the entire body in his delivery of the ball; therefore the entire body must be stretched and warmed up. The stretches should not be done while the body is "cold." My trainees ride their bikes to my gym or jog, which warms up the muscles.

There are several stretches which should not be done because they place harsh strain on the joints rather than on the muscle mass which stretching is designed to relax. The trainee should never feel the strain of connective tissue on the bone joint.

The Hurdler Stretch is one of the worst stretches the athletes do improperly, though many coaches instruct their athletes to use this exercise. It is very destabilizing to the knee joint and can cause knee problems as the athlete matures, along with the added strain of the athletic contest.

To identify the muscles mentioned here, refer to the diagrams following Chapter One. I have referred to the stretching exercises described here in figure numbers in an S series.

See Figures S-1 through S-14 for correct methods used by Maitland Sports Training. Notice that a trainee may appear to be stretching a single limb though he is stretching many adjacent muscles. This saves time while completely stretching all the muscles. I recommend Bob Anderson's "Book of Stretching" for those desiring a complete program of stretching for all sports and recreational activities.

In addition to the conditioning stretches. I have included stretches for batting warm ups. I see many ballplayers place the "donut" on the bat and begin swinging the bat just prior to going to the plate. I feel this is wrong as the weight training should be done at least twenty-four hours prior to game time (with light weights). The reaction of the muscles worked with the donut is to begin recovery immediately after the weight has worked them. Thus the muscles retract and are tightening up at a time when they should be relaxed and able to reach for the "hit" on the ball.

Figures S-1 and S-2 - Anterior deltoid stretch (front shoulder)

Figure S-1   Figure S-2

Figure S-1 shows the Anterior Deltoid (front shoulder) Stretch. Grab a stationary object and turn away from the object with your palms facing outward. Hold for twenty seconds and do the same with the other arm. Do not overstretch causing pain or strain.

Figure S-2 shows the Biceps, Posterior Deltoid, and Lumbar (lower back) stretches. It will also stretch the latissimus dorsi (upper back behind the chest).

Figures S-3 and S-4 and S-5 and S-6

Figure S-3   Figure S-4

Figure S-3 shows the Hamstring (large muscle behind the legs) Stretch. This method stretches the torso as well as the gluteus maximus (large muscle above the hamstring). Do each side for twenty seconds.

Figure S-4 shows the Trunk and Shoulder Stretch. Hold for twenty seconds each side.

Figure S-6

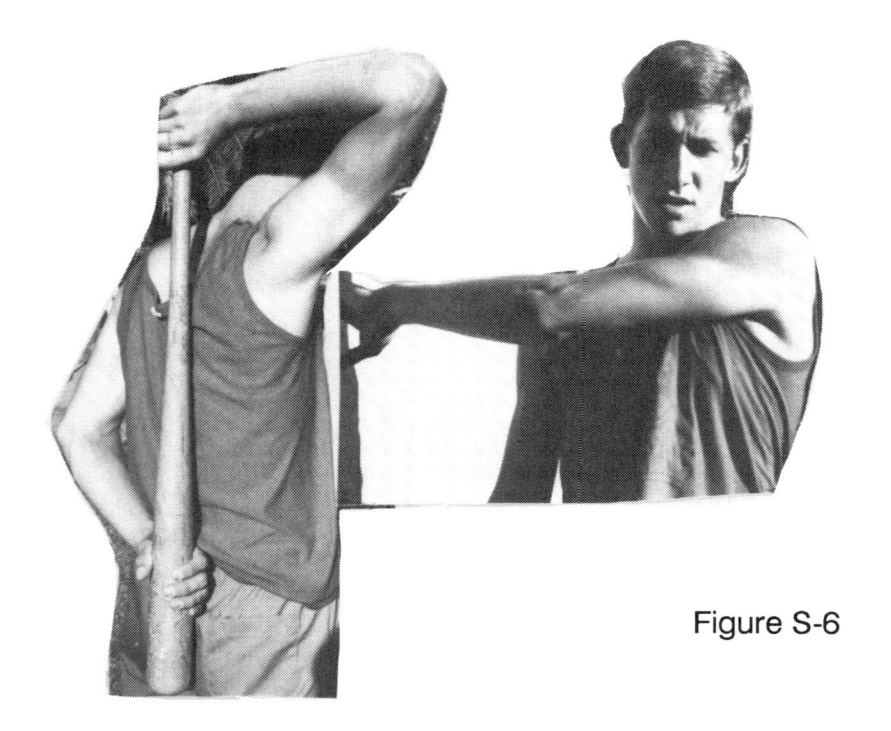

Figure S-5

Figure S-5 shows the Triceps (muscle behind the upper arm) and Wind-up Stretch. Hold for twenty seconds each arm. It also stretches the minor pectoralis (upper chest) and the external obliques (stomach muscles to the front side).

Figure S-6 shows the Posterior Deltoid (rear shoulder muscle) Stretch. Place fingers on object and turn body toward the arm being worked. Hold for twenty seconds each arm.

Figures S-7 through S-14 show the stretches the author has his trainees use before every weight training session. If the author is coaching an athletic team he will add stretches for that particular sport. In this book, you will see the baseball stretches used by the author in training pitchers.

Figures S-7 and S-8

Figure S-7 shows a stretch that stretches the rib cage as well as the deltoids, triceps, biceps, obliques, and spinae erectors (muscles to the back side above the hip bone) and the leg muscles. Notice that the palms are turned out to force the rib cage and arms to stretch as an entire unit which includes the legs. Hold on to each side for twenty seconds. This is an excellent stretch for batting and throwing.

Figure S-8 shows the move from S-7 to the Hamstring Stretch in this illustration. The lumbar region is stretched as well as the calf and adductor muscles of the leg. Again we are stretching the rib cage and the deltoids as well as the pectoralis minor and the latissimus dorsi. The minute muscles of the wrist and lower arm are being worked also.

When you work with youngsters who are in a hurry to get on with the fun (most find stretching boring), it's good to have stretches that can accomplish many tasks for the growing body at once. This cuts down on the time but allows the safe stretching of all muscle groups.

Figures S-9 and S-10

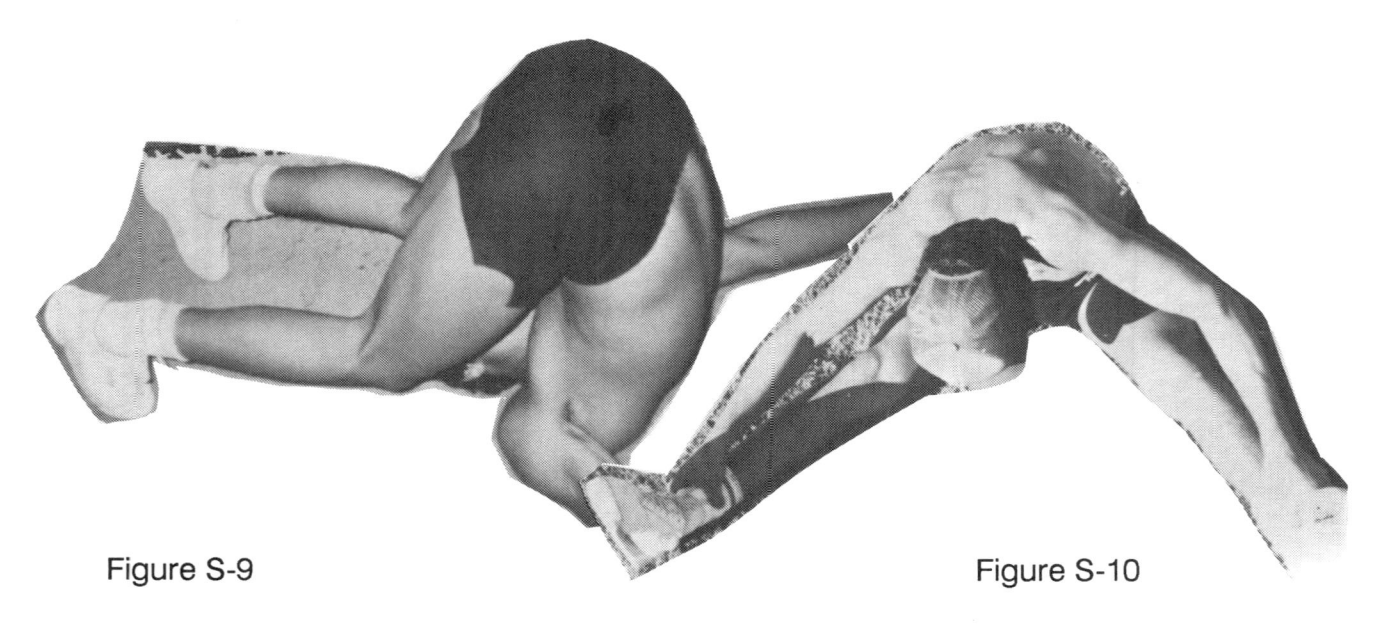

Figure S-9   Figure S-10

Figure S-9 shows the Gluteal-Spinal Stretch. It also stretches the hamstrings and the trapezius muscles. Many trainers forget the minute muscles of the neck (trapezius) and upper shoulder. Many young trainees come to me complaining of a sore neck due to some school activity that occurred that day. They were not prepared for the activity and were not able to continue their day without stretch therapy.

Notice that the trainee in Figure S-9 uses his arms to steady his body in this stretch. His feet are not touching the floor. They are being held above the floor, allowing for a good stretch in the areas described. The more he straightens his legs, the more stretch he will experience in the hamstring and gluteal area. Hold for twenty seconds.

Figure S-10 shows Bobby Valenzuela doing the Hamstring-Adductor-Spinal Stretch. Notice Bobby is running his hands down his legs to enhance the stretching of the upper body with the arms and deltoids. Hold for twenty seconds.

Figure S-11 and S-12

Figure S-11. Bobby Valenzuela (above) is doing the alternative Hamstring stretch with legs together. This can be used if the trainee is suffering adductor or groin injury. It also stretches the Spinal Column.

Figure S-12 (right). Shows Bill Behm in the Quadricep stretch. Injuries can occur if the "Quads" are not stretched in correct proportion to the "Hamstring." One muscle can overpower another causing a "pulled" hamstring.

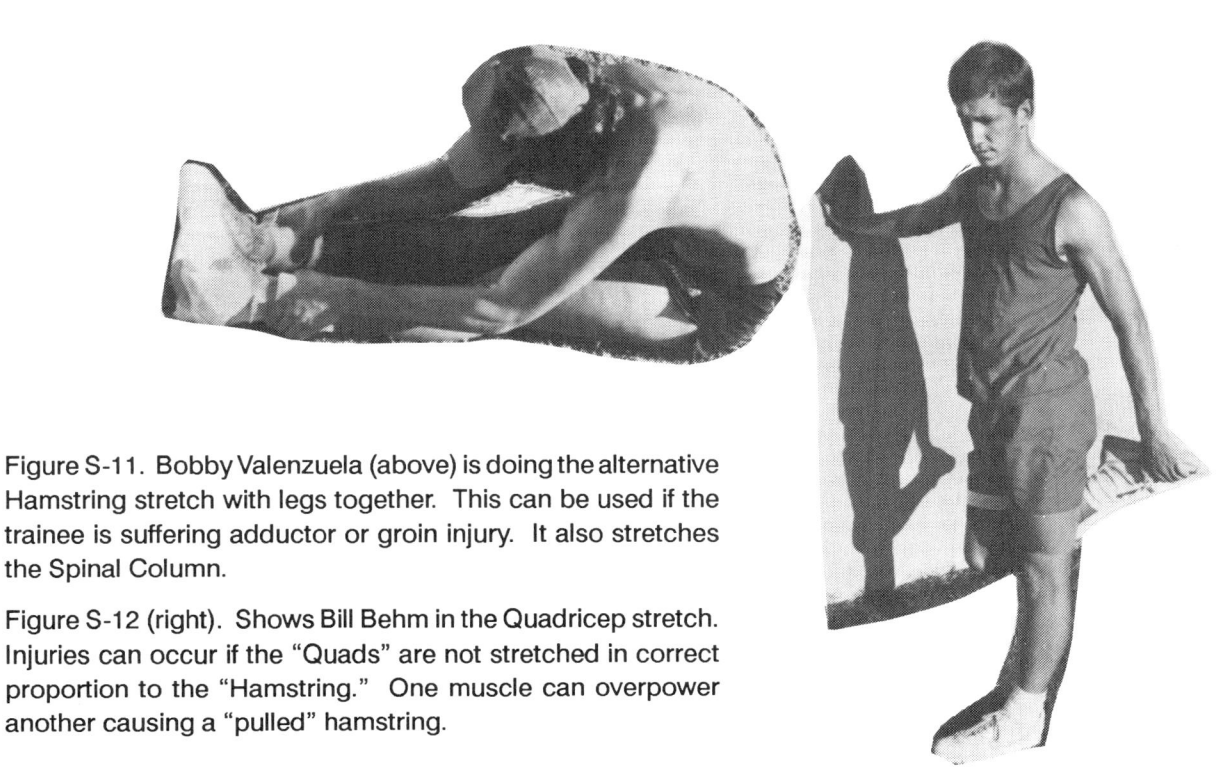

Figure S-11 shows another Hamstring Spinal Stretch with legs closed to concentrate the action on the spinal column and the hamstrings. The adductors are not involved in this stretch. Hold all stretches for twenty seconds. This stretch may be substituted for the S-10 stretch if the trainee has a pulled adductor or groin muscle.

Figure S-12 shows the Quadriceps Stretch (muscle opposite the hamstring). Injuries can occur in the hamstring area if the opposing muscle (quadriceps) is not stretched or worked in the proper proportion. The coach/instructor must be aware of the ratio of work done by the trainee and ensure one area does not overcome the opposing muscle group by overwork or improper stretching techniques. This manner of stretching also stretches the soleus and the patellar ligaments (calf and knee tendons).

Notice Bill Behm is using the opposite arm to hold the opposing leg. This manner has an added therapeutic value of placing the proper stress on the femoris muscle group-tendon of quadriceps (muscle group above the knee in the middle) and the vastus medialis (inside muscle group above the knee) to properly align the aforementioned areas. This allows for the stabilization of that crucial area for many years to come.

Figure S-13 Calf stretches

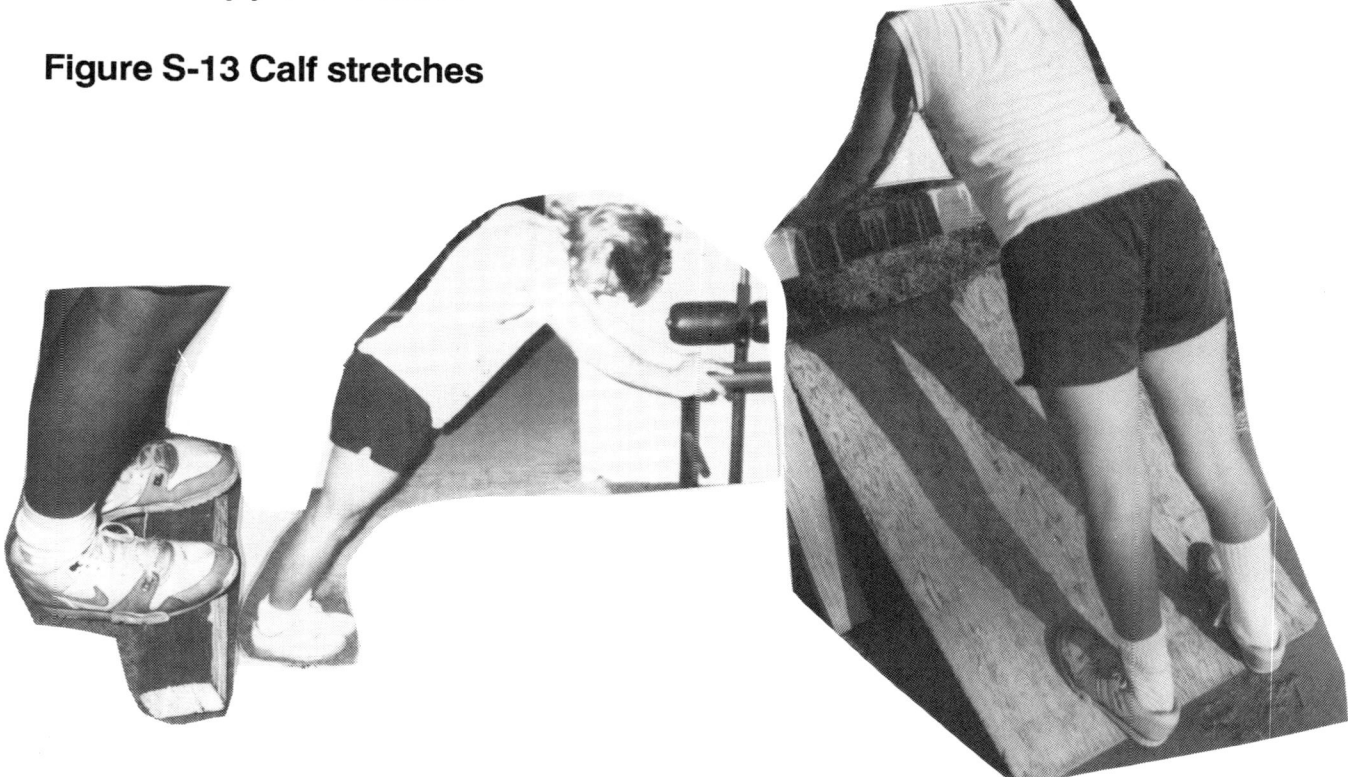

Figure 13. The calf stretch done three ways

In Figure S-12, Bill allows the quadricep to slowly "give way" as the muscle relaxes. All stretching should be done with care and the muscle given time to relax naturally. Do not force the muscle to the point of pain. The muscle should feel a little discomfort (says Bob Anderson in his "Book of Stretching") that diminishes as the body relaxes. If too much force or too little time is allowed, the muscle may suffer a strain or sprain after some use. The athlete may not know the cause. The cause can be the incorrect technique in the warm up stretching period. See Bill in Figure S-12 for the correct Quadriceps Stretch.

Figure S-13 also shows various methods of stretching the calf muscle (gastrocnemius) located behind the lower leg above the ankle. This is the area that usually hurts the most after running when you are not in shape. This stretch also works the Achilles tendon located behind the ankles above the heels. This area can be damaged from improper stretching as well as from running in improperly fitted or poorly designed athletic shoes. Aerobics in clubs and schools have caused damage to trainees of all ages because they were done on hard surfaces with no give. Since many school children cannot afford the high-priced athletic shoes, much harm is done to the knees and ankles as well as to the Achilles tendon. Many of these injuries are not reversible, and the youth is injured for life or prone to constant injuries in those areas.

MORE ON IMPROPER STRETCHES

At the beginning of this chapter, I mentioned the harm done by the Hurdler's Stretch. The Hurdler's Stretch is an attempt to work and loosen the adductor longus (large muscle inside the leg that pulls the legs together between the quadriceps and hamstring muscle) to allow for greater movement of the legs laterally without pulling the muscle.

In Figure S-14 we see Bobby demonstrating the proper method to stretch the same muscles without the destabilizing pressure on the patellar tendons and the vastus medialis which keep the patella in proper alignment preventing hyper-extension. We can readily see the safety in using the stretch as in Figure S-14. Notice the quadriceps and the patellar tendons are being worked along with the adductors. The proper performance of the Hurdler's Stretch is shown in S-14.

If the readers would like corroboration of the stretch facts I have given I urge them to read the article on this subject in the October/November 1984 issue of the "National Strength and Conditioning Association Journal." I have personally copied the article and distributed it to high school and Pop Warner and various baseball organizations and yet I still see young athletes being forced to perform these harmful stretches.

64

**Figures S-14 (left) and S-15 (right) proper/improper stretch
Bottom left - proper hurdler stretch.**

Figure 14.   Proper stretches Top and bottom. left. Hurdler stretch without injury.

Figure 15. Improper hurdler stretch

In Figure 15, notice the outstretched bent leg with pressure laterally applied to the patellar tendons by the further extension of the tibia (lower leg below knee and above ankle). This pressure is what destabilizes the knee. The effect would be the same if you tried to make your finger bend sideways (laterally) rather than to bend and work the way it is supposed to do. Try to bend your finger to the side. When you notice pain, stop. You will realize the finger does not bend that way. With the leg in the same predicament, some feel the pain is part of "getting in shape." Instructors teach their impressionable students the false adage, "No pain, no gain."

Also in Figure S-15 notice Bobby's left leg is stretched straight out. This is stretching the hamstring muscle group. This can be accomplished by using the stretch as shown in Figure S-11. Or, if the adductors and the hamstrings need work, you may use the stretch as in Figure S-10 or Figure S-14.

Figures S-16 and S-17 - Improper hurdler stretch - Improper patellar tendon stretch.

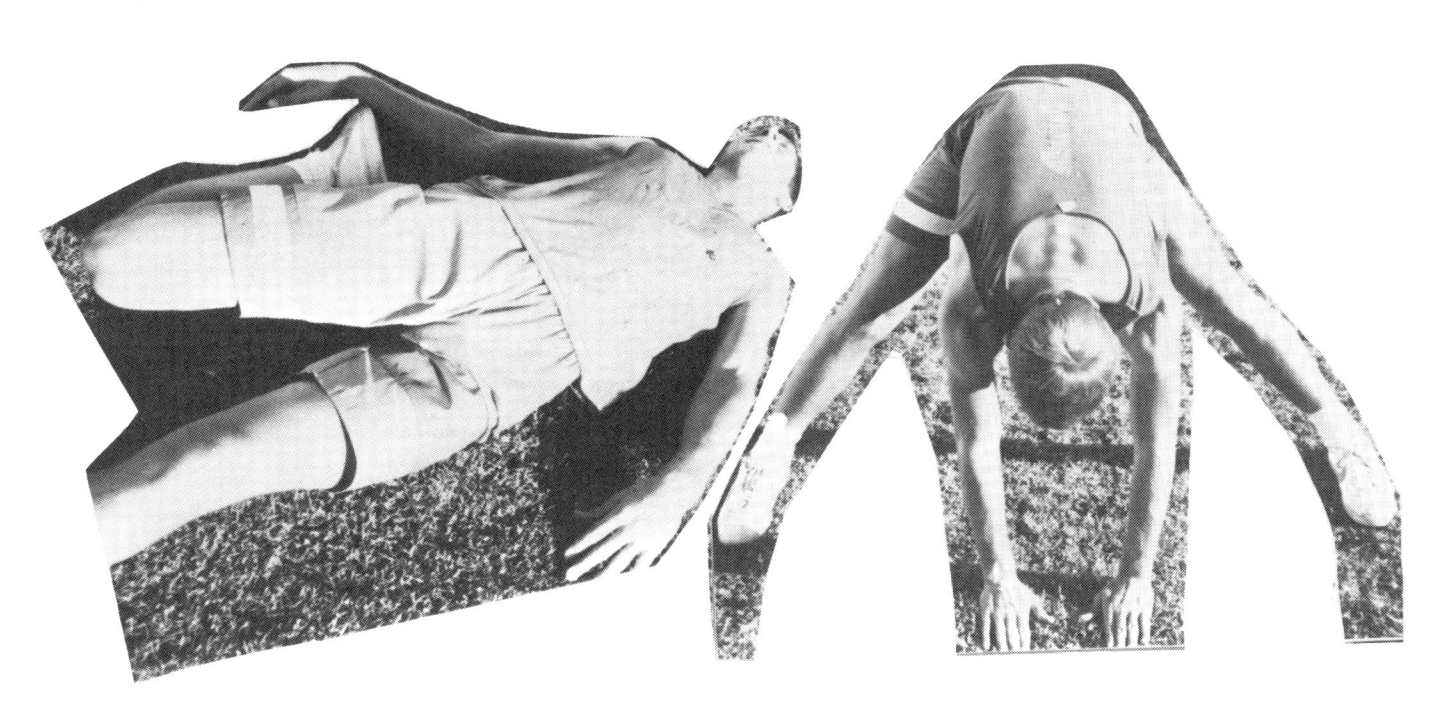

Figure S-16 Improper Hurdler Stretches

Figure S-17. Improper attempt at hamstring stretch

In Figures S-16 and S-17 you see other stretches that are harmful to the stability of the knee and ankles. Notice Bill's right leg (bent) being forced to support the weight of his one hundred eighty pound body. Imagine the stress on the knee, quadriceps group as well as the tibial tendons and the ankle. Needless to say, Bill asked that I hurry and get the picture quickly as he was in much pain. Yet there are adults who teach their students (both adult and children) that this is a proper and safe method. To accomplish the same stretching goals without the harm and pain, I refer the reader to Figure S-12. This shows the safe method to stretch the same muscle group including the tibial tendons.

Figure S-17 shows the trainee attempting to stretch the spinal column and the hamstrings and adductors. This method may not look as harmful as it is, but notice the stress on the patellar ligaments again. Growing bodies need time to mature and to become strong in the proper alignment. Placing stress over a period of time (usually years as in the case of children) can cause a misalignment due to weakening of the supporting connective tissue in the knee area as well as in the ankles. The desirable results can be obtained with no stress by using the methods described in Figures S-9, S-10, and S-11 if a spinal column stretch is sought.

This concludes the chapter on stretching. The reader is encouraged to take stretching as a serious part of the training program. Many athletes have suffered long terms on the bench because they did not pay attention to pre-game or pre-training warm ups and stretches. Adult coaches and instructors as well as parents should be aware of the proper methods in stretching, as well as training for any athletic event. I know of a few youngsters who wished they had paid attention to stretching. They've spent much of their parents' money and time for corrective therapy with a sports doctor because they hurried through the warm up session of the training program or they were not instructed property.

The best training machines and methods will not substitute for a good pre-training warm up and stretching session. The stretching and warm up can serve also as mental disciplining. Your mind has to be in the workouts to get the most benefit from the sessions.

CHAPTER XVI

WEIGHT TRAINING PROGRAM FOR PITCHERS AND BATTERS

PROGRAM TWO

This section of the book is dedicated to the young athlete and presents the use of weight training as a method of strengthening those muscles most concerned with throwing. The exercises can be used for developing a strong throw for infielders and outfielders alike. However, since the book is geared to the pitcher, the exercises will be discussed as though I were training a pitcher.

The exercises in this series which I have marked W are presented in a manner that indicates the benefits in power hitting also. Many of the muscles worked for throwing will also aid in the power of the batter. Workout days are Monday-Wednesday-Friday or Tuesday-Thursday-Saturday or Sunday-Tuesday-Thursday. Other days you rest and engage in aerobic fun activities.

REASON FOR "PROGRAM TWO" STARTING THIS WORKOUT

As mentioned earlier, this book is the second of a series of three special weight training programs for athletes. The first book is "Beginning Weight Training For Young Athletes." That book is called Program One. I have numbered the programs in this way so the parent and teacher-coach may be aware of the levels of difficulty of each program. Program One is "Beginner" only. Even though this book "Young Ballplayer's Guide To Safe Pitching Ages Eight Through Adult," concentrates on a special sport, it still starts from Beginner and goes on through Advanced.

The third book is for older advanced youngsters ages fourteen through adult. It is called *Weight Training for Gifted Athletes — Ages 14 through Adult.* It is a co-educational program for conditioning and weight training with stretches, nutrition, and aspects of plyometric and mental training. It is an excellent, complete program for in-season and off-season recreational or athletic program. Baseballers may use this book (Program III) for off season training if they are advanced and experienced and have completed and understood the other two programs.

WORKOUT DAY ONE

Figure W-1. - Dumbbell benchpress-3x12 Twist wrist as you raise dumbbell

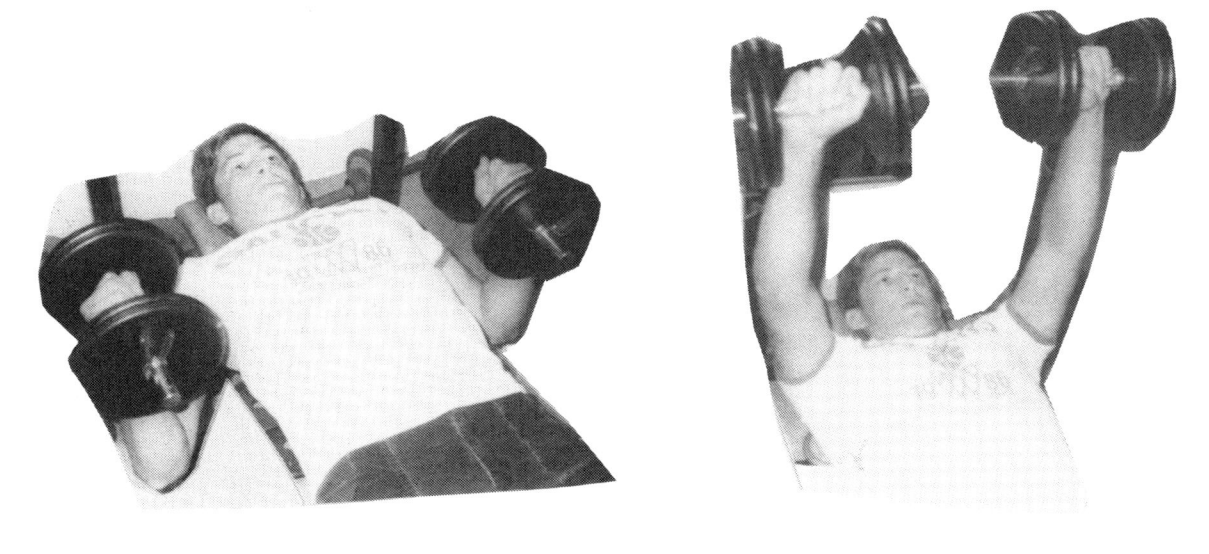

Start   Finish

This exercise is excellent for stretching the chest muscles (pectoralis) and working the lower triceps (back of upper arm). It also strengthens the ligaments of the deltoids (shoulders) which aid in holding the arm and shoulder joint (rotator cuff) in place. Move the dumbbells as far below the chest as possible to feel a good stretch and a good push on the chest and triceps. Completed movements are very important. (Notice wrist twist.)

If you are not familiar with the jargon of the weight room, the phrase "sets of repetitions" means count the repetitions of an exercise, rest at least twenty seconds and then repeat the specified number of times to do the exercise (reps). Each time you do this number is a set. Thus three sets of twelve repetitions means that the trainee does the exercise twelve times, then rests, and does the same thing two more times — thus three sets of twelve, shortened to 3x12. The last exercise movement is done as properly and fully as the first movement.

You should use a weight that offers enough resistance without tiring you or overstraining the muscles on the last rep of the set.

Baseball players do not need to work with heavy weights. They will gain the speed and endurance needed for play by using light to medium weights with high reps. This will develop speed and endurance.

Figure W-2. Clean to shoulders- 3x10

Begin   Midpoint (pull)   End (To shoulder)

Keep your arm straight when you squat down with back straight. Grab the barbell and raise using your legs (not your back) and throw the weight to the upper chest area.

The Clean To Shoulders allows the entire body to enter into the muscle and strength coordination. It develops the deltoids (shoulders), obliques and spinae flexors and erectors (stomach) as well as the quadriceps (front leg muscle). The forearms and wrists are also strengthened. I cannot think of a better exercise for an athlete, no matter what his sport. This exercise utilizes about 34 percent of the total muscle mass of the body. Coupled with the arm and wrist action and upper back and chest involvement, it can utilize as much as 54 percent of the total body muscle mass.

The athlete will feel stronger over his entire body if he uses this exercise properly and cautiously in his training regimen. Remember, the pitcher and the batter use the entire body for throwing and hitting. This exercise will coordinate the massive power and strength of the muscles in action.

Figure W-3. Dumbbell Shoulder Shrug (with dumbbell or barbell) 3x12

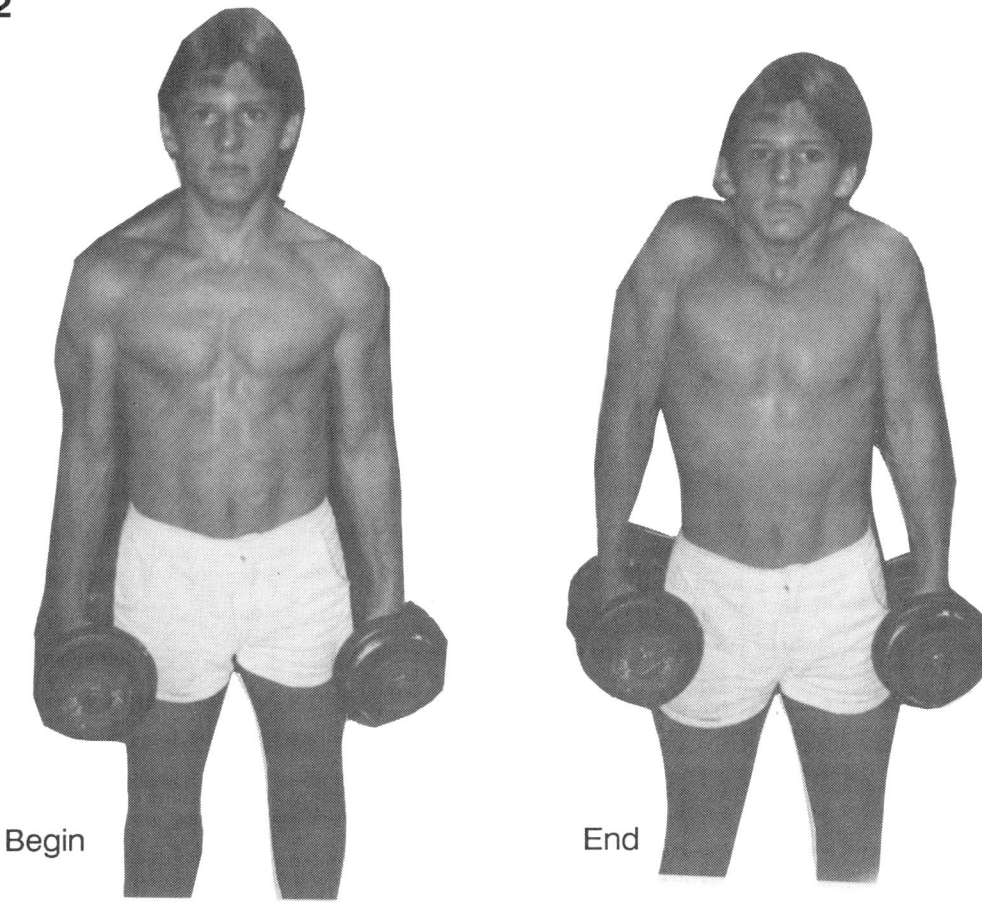

Begin   End

The shoulders move up and down without jerking. Use heavier weights that allow a good workout and good movement. The Shoulder Shrug builds the trapezius (lower neck) muscle. The muscle aids in strengthening the connective tissue of the upper back (scapular and rhomboid) and middle shoulder area (medial deltoid). My trainees perform this exercise between reps of the next exercise.

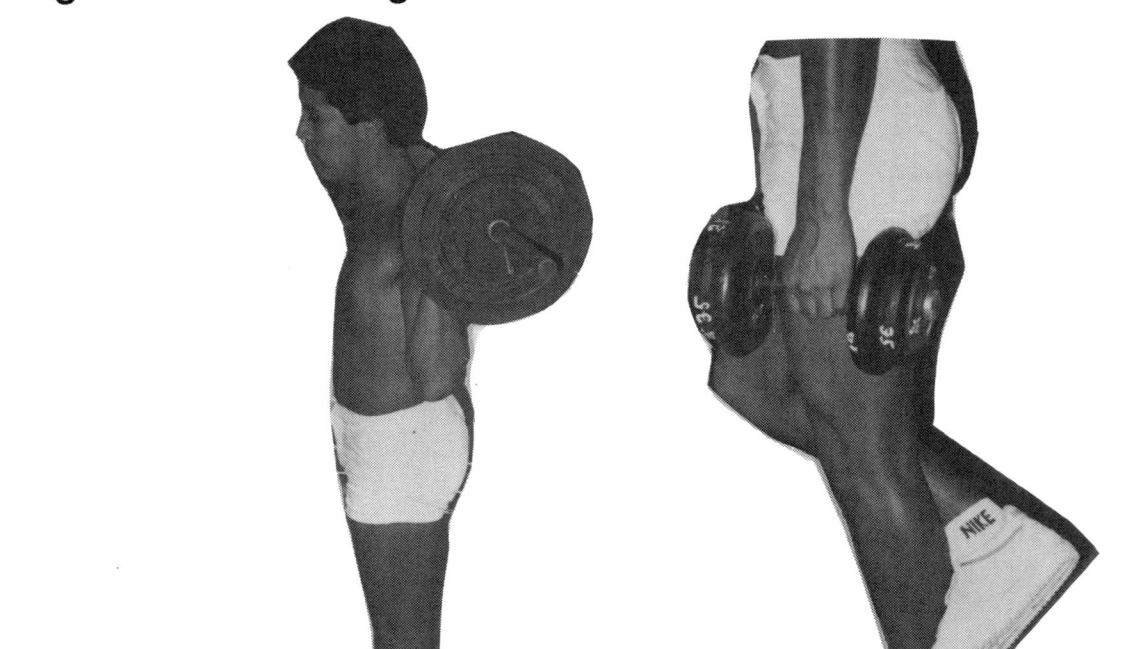

Figure W-4. - Standing Calf Raise - 3x12

Begin
Barbell

End
Dumbbell

Use one leg with dumbbell on a 2x4 or door stoop — 2 legs balanced on the 2x4 with barbell or light to medium weight.

The Standing Calf Raise offers the most movement for the Achilles tendon and ankle and calf support tendons. It also uses the entire support system of the quadriceps and the hamstrings. The Standing Calf Raise should be done in alternate reps with the Shoulder Shrug (Figure W-3) to save time. Since neither exercise is physiologically taxing nor similar in muscle exertion requirements, they are ideal for a "circuiting" approach. That is, do one set of 3x12 of Shoulder Shrugs, and then do one set of Standing Calf Raises and alternate each until three sets of the Shrugs and two sets of sixteen of the Standing Calf Raises are completed. Move the heels all the way down and all the way up. The foot is placed on the 2x4 just behind the joint of the toes and foot.

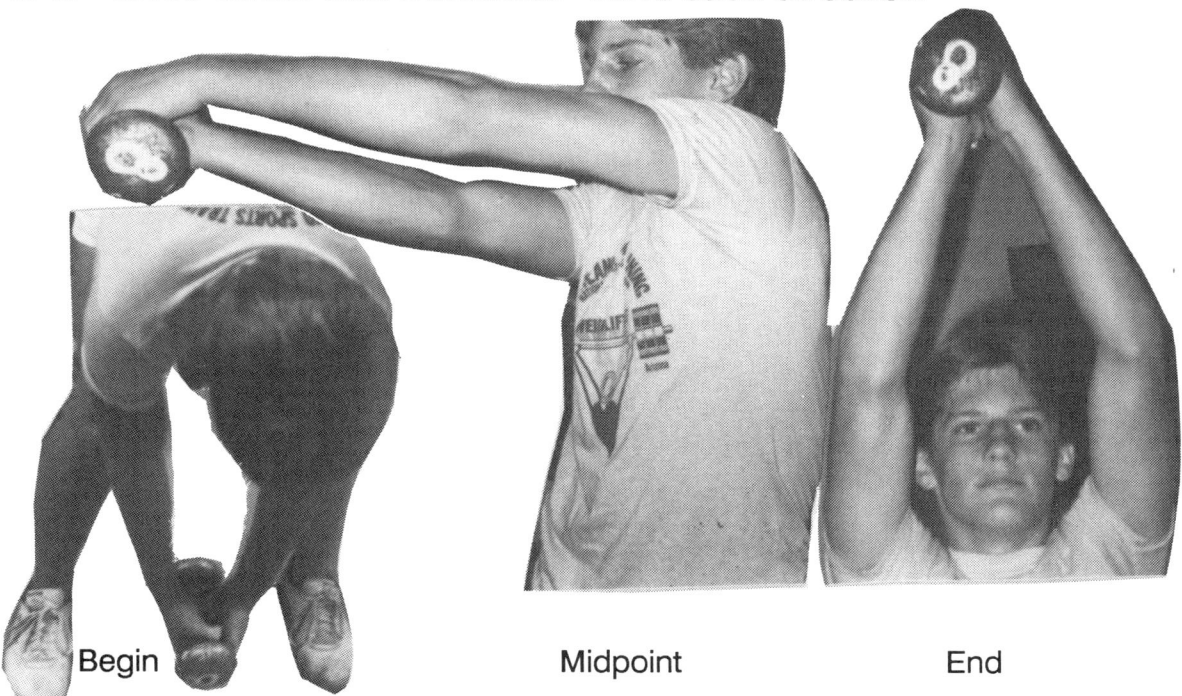

Figure W-5. - Torso Circle with Dumbbell - 2x16 each direction

Begin   Midpoint   End

The Torso Circle is not one of my trainees' favorite exercises. They do come to appreciate it when they discover the added strength and dexterity of the torso area as well as the coordination of the legs with the movement of the torso. The weight is held down as pictured in Figure W-5, then raised in circular motion over the head and down the opposite side while twisting the wrist. The palm holding the weight should be pointed toward the ceiling as the arm moves to the upward motion. The legs are not stiff. They move in a circular motion as the dumbbell circles around the body. This exercise will mimic many of the moves required in most ball game situations. The weight strengthens the spinae erectors, spinae flexors (stomach and side muscles) as well as the quadriceps, calves, and hamstrings.

The exercise allows the body to stretch and strengthen the spinal column as well as the other areas mentioned. It can assist the body speed in "coming around" on the pitched ball when batting, or getting the body "into the pitch" when you are throwing. At first you will feel a tightening of the spinae erectors and the external obliques (alongside the stomach); however, as you get into better shape this tightness will stop and you will enjoy a freedom of movement and dexterity unknown to you.

Figure W-6. - Standing Press Squat (dumbbell) - 3x10

Begin   End

This exercise is particularly good for developing the power needed in throwing. It allows the trainee to combine the benefits of the squat, which uses about 31 percent of the total body muscle mass, as well as the benefits of the press. To begin exercise, select dumbbells that will allow you to complete three sets of ten repetitions without overtiring or straining the muscles.

Hold the dumbbells slightly in front of the shoulders with the palms pointed toward each other as you go down into a squat without moving the dumbbells. Once your quadriceps are about parallel with the floor, begin completing the squat and raise the body upward while raising (pressing) the dumbbells overhead. While you are raising the dumbbells, you are twisting your wrist so your dumbbells reach the topmost point overhead with the palms facing away from the body, toward the front.

This exercise develops the power of the legs as well as the upper body, arms, and wrist. It allows coordination and strengthening of those muscles used in throwing. It is also a time saver in that two areas are trained at the same time.

Baseball is a sport that takes up time; so exercises can be of a nature to combine various muscle groups to accomplish a desired goal quickly and safely. Once the trainee learns the basics of the program, he/she may elect to "circuit" certain exercises as in the Shrug and Calf Raise.

Figure W-7. - Barbell and Dumbbell Strict Curl - 3x12

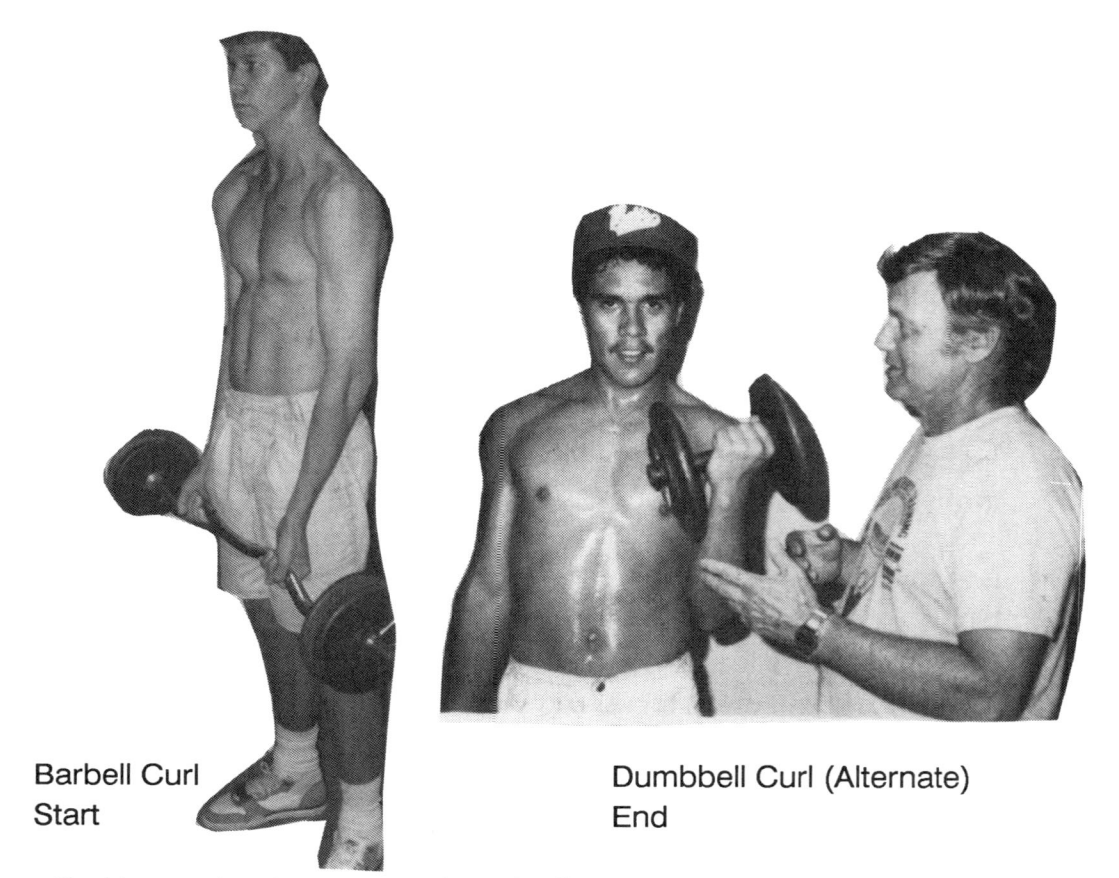

Barbell Curl
Start

Dumbbell Curl (Alternate)
End

The Strict Arm Curl has to be done correctly to facilitate the entire upper body in training. Most trainees are surprised to learn that the Strict Arm Curl works the pectoralis minor (upper chest), as well as the trapezius (neck), deltoids (shoulders), scapular, and other back muscles. You will also feel the spinae flexors and obliques working to stabilize the trunk area of your body. Your wrists and forearms will feel the work also. To enhance the wrist action, the wrist should be rotated as you move up and down. There is no need to use heavy weights as you will feel the muscles working with a light to medium weight with the high reps.

Remember, for a sport such as baseball, we use light to medium weights with high fast reps to enhance strength and speed.

Figure W-8. - Dumbbell or Barbell Tricep Extension - 3x12

Begin
Barbell

End
Dumbbell

The Triceps Extension builds strength in the area of the upper arm behind the biceps muscle. You will feel more ability to power your throw with less effort when this area is trained properly. Care should be taken to prevent overextending the epiphysis (elbow joint). If the trainee hurries through this exercise, damage may result due to the sudden jerking of the area described. This is a very important part of the body for any recreational or sporting activity.

The trainee should feel his/her way through the full range of movement, stopping just short of reaching the full extension of the arm. The slight bend of the elbow at completion will prevent the straining and possible overextension of the arm.

Figure W-9. - Wrist Curl Palms Up (barbbell) - 3x10

Start   End

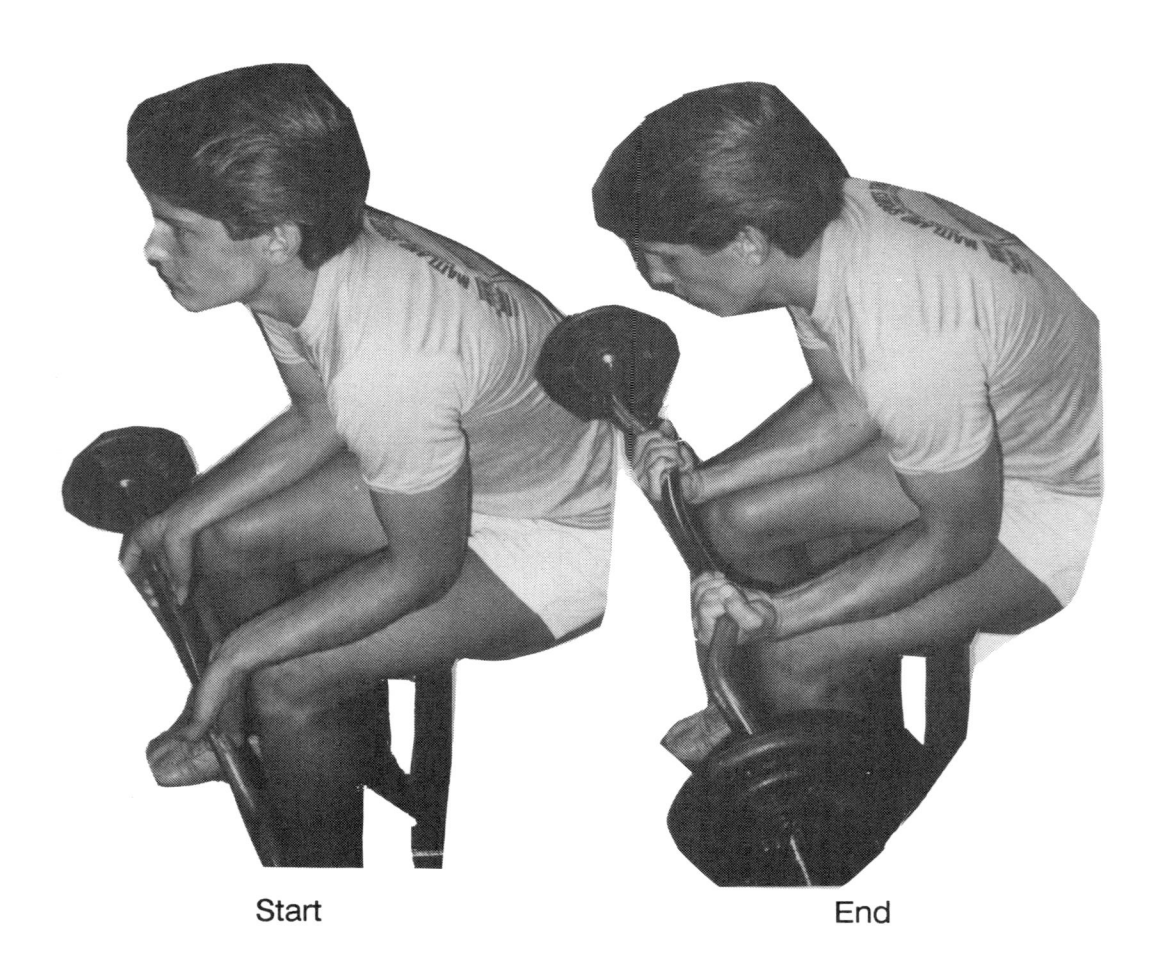

It will be apparent what this exercise is to accomplish. It will develop flexor and extensors of the lower arm and the power of the wrist and fingers. They all lead to a stronger grip for the ball and power to the bat. You will feel the muscles of the flexors tightening as you allow the barbell to roll down the fingers, and roll the fingers back up, curling the wrist all the way up toward your body to complete the movement.

Figure W-10. - Jump Rope - 100 times forward

Jump Rope

There is no greater value than the Jump Rope for developing calves, hamstrings, quadriceps, and Achilles tendon strength.

My trainees are taught to run in place as the feet alternate over the rope. The child may have a grace period of a couple of sessions where he/she may learn to coordinate the movement of the rope under the feet.

The alternating feet enhance the autonomic nervous system's ability to react with little or no conscious effort. It increases speed and agility while forcing the lower extremities to enjoy a burst of rapid development and quick strength.

As the trainees become proficient in the forward jump, they should learn the backward Jump Rope as well. Needless to say how much this ability would enhance the total body awareness of action in the field.

The Jump Rope is labeled as a plyometric exercise because it enhances the muscle's ability to react quickly, and the brain message paths to the myelin sheaths of the nerve fibers are quickened. Please see the February-March 1987 issue of the "National Strength and Conditioning Association Journal." It discusses the merits of the jump rope in detail.

The first day's training is completed. You should not throw the baseball (i.e. pitch) the same day you weight train. The days you are to pitch should be used to form the mental image you want in the game. In fact, mental imaging is a good mental exercise to use while you are stretching properly.

WORKOUT DAY TWO

Figure W-11. - Incline Dumbbell Benchpress - 3x10

Start   End

On the last workout day, we used the flat bench to work the major chest muscles (pectoralis major). Today we are using the slant bench to work the minor pectoralis (upper chest muscles). The result will be a greater strength in the entire deltoid (shoulder), latissimus dorsi (back) and scapular (upper back) areas as well as the upper chest. These muscles act as the major support muscles (along with the latissimus dorsi) in helping the shoulder and upper back muscles deliver strength and power to throw (and hit when batting).

Lie on your back holding the dumbbells as far down as you can. Allow the dumbbells to stretch the chest (pectoralis) until you feel it. After the stretch, push the dumbbells up while twisting the wrist so the palms face out (away from the body) as you complete the motion.

Please allow complete movement in both directions. Do not straighten your elbow when reaching the top of the movement. Always keep your elbow slightly bent upon reaching the uppermost point of the press. This habit will prevent injuries to the growth plates in that area (epiphysis). Do three sets of ten.

If the youth is inexperienced or not as yet mature enough physically, the weights should be lowered to allow completion of as many reps as he/she can safely complete without overstraining. The youth should have moderate difficulty on the last repetition when done correctly. If the youth is having difficulty on the second set, eighth repetition, he/she should stop and work at this level until strength and endurance are increased or the child matures.

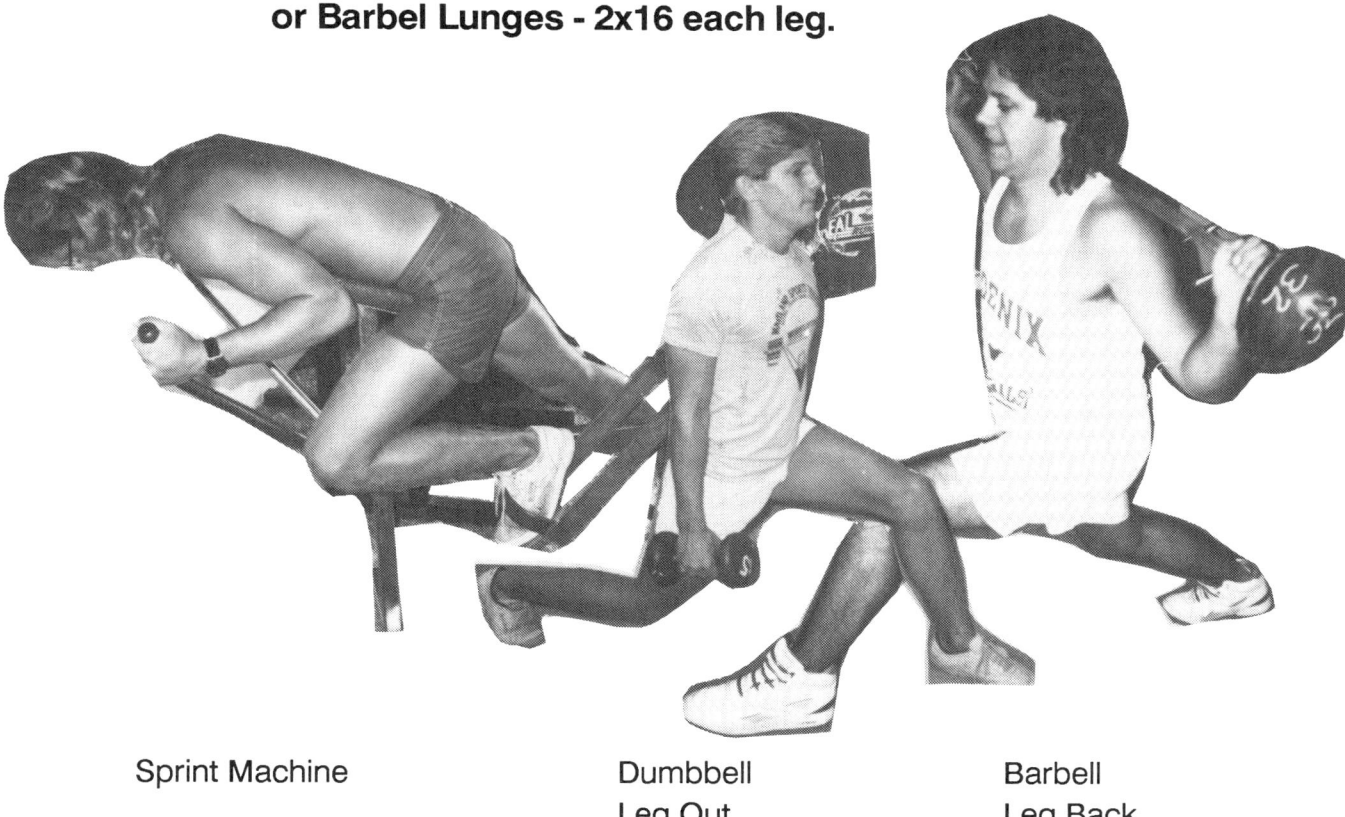

Figure W-12. - Sprint Maching-100 each Leg or Dumbbell Lunges (barbell may be used if experienced) - 12x16 each leg or Barbel Lunges - 2x16 each leg.

Sprint Machine   Dumbbell   Barbell
                     Leg Out   Leg Back

I was able to purchase a used sprint machine from the Olympic Fitness Equipment store in town for under $100. The young athletes seem to be motivated to use it. The machine offers a safe and effective method of working the quadriceps (front leg muscles) and strengthening the patellar tendons (tendons that hold the knee cap in place; remember, patella is another word for knee cap). The youngsters seem to enjoy working on the machine which I have seen in most high schools and professional gyms or health clubs a few years ago.

Since most homes do not have the sprint machine, I have demonstrated the dumbbell and barbell use in the lunge exercise. With the dumbbells, you hold as shown in the picture and alternate legs in a jumping motion if you are experienced, capable, and desire a very quick strength and stamina builder. If the youngster is not experienced, he/she may alternately place one foot in front leaving the other to the rear.

The youth then sets the feet apart so as to feel a pleasant stretch in the hamstring (back of leg) while the quadriceps (upper front of leg) is parallel to the floor. The body is then forced to push off the front leg to an upright position and the rear leg is placed to the rear. The motion is performed for two sets of sixteen repetitions.

The same exercise can be performed with a barbell across the shoulders. The youngster should be experienced, and spotted with the barbell, as many trainees tend to lean forward while performing the exercise. The leg movements are the same as in using the dumbbells. The barbell requires more care in balancing and requires more strictness in performing the work.

Do not overload the trainee. The exercise should be done in a full movement allowing for a good strong push to the transfer point of the rear leg. Two sets of sixteen repetitions allow for a good workout without undue strain on the Achilles tendon (rear of ankle) or the patella (knee cap).

Figure W-13. - Thigh Curl - Machine - Free Weights - 3x10

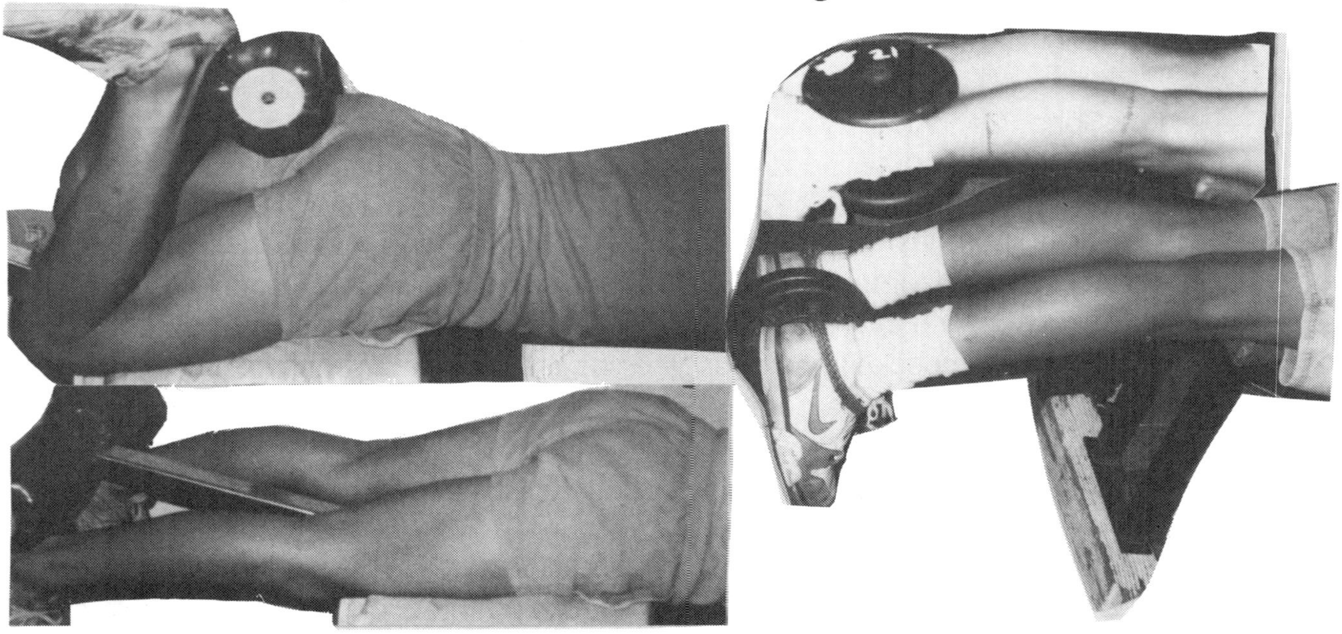

Bottom: Begin thigh curl
Top: End machine
         Thigh Curl

Using free weights
for Thigh Curl

The Thigh Curl works the muscle on the backside of the leg, the hamstring muscle. It is odd that the exercise is called the Thigh Curl because the thigh is to the front of the muscle being curled. You will feel the work and the strength develop in the hamstring area behind the leg. Three sets of ten reps allow the muscle to work without overloading. Fewer reps can cause the youth to build bulk, which is not what is needed at this stage of strength and conditioning for baseball.

As the picture shows, lie on your stomach with the legs straight and the arms outstretched to offer support in the raising stage of the exercise. Allow the weight to raise to 90 degrees with the machine and a little less when using the leg weights. (The leg weights may fall if brought to 90 degrees or more.) On the completion of the "pull," the legs should be controlled in the downward movement so as to prevent damage to the patellar tendons and ligaments.

Figure W-14. - Machine Leg Extension-Leg weights or Dumbbell Leg Extension -

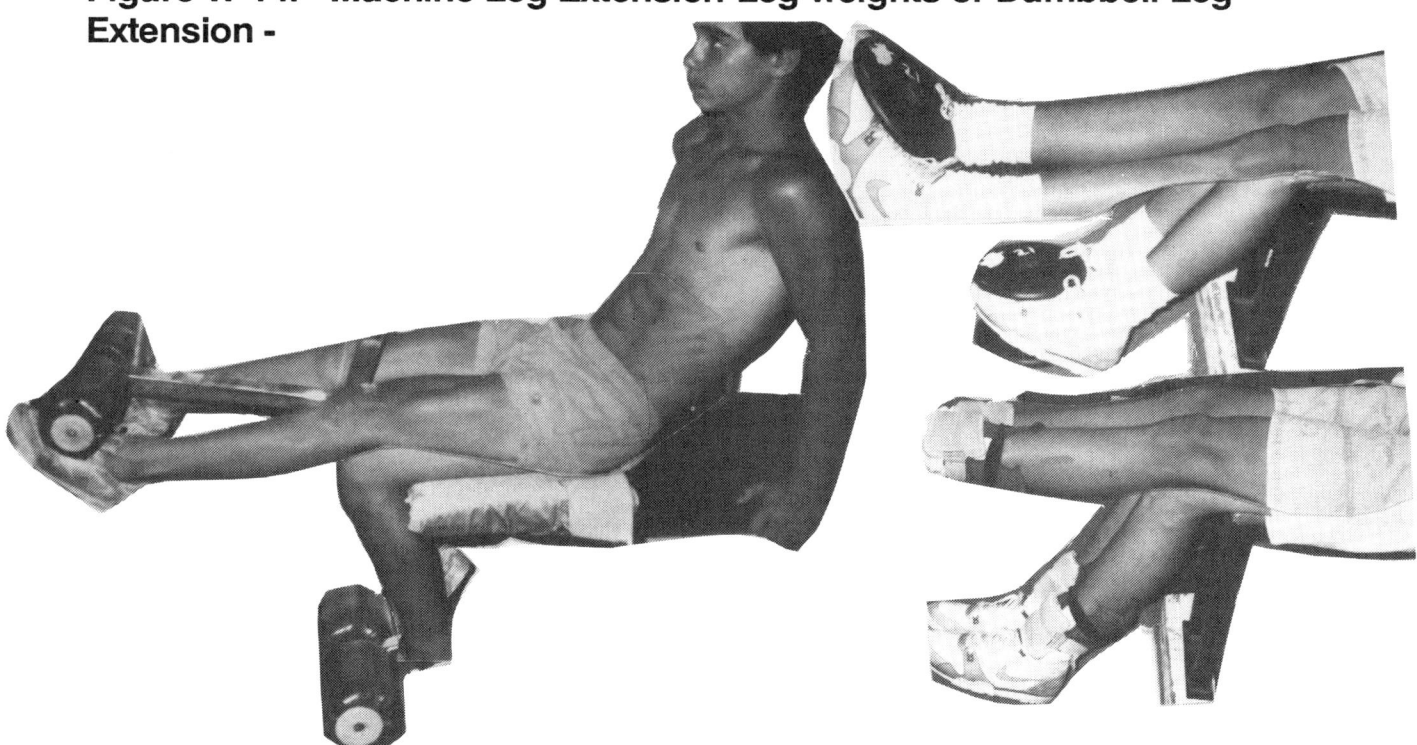

Machine Leg Extension
Begin: begin and end

Leg Extension with Dumbbell
or 10 pound ankle weights
on slanted bench

This exercise will work the muscle opposite the hamstring. You will feel the strength developing in the front of the leg (quadriceps). You will feel the muscles around the patella (knee) working very hard. The knee is a very important joint to the athlete and should be worked to strengthen the supporting tendons and muscles. Do not cause harmful strain by doing too much weight or by sloppy execution.

If you were to do leg extensions without the opposite muscle being worked in the Thigh Curl in the course of the same week, the knee would become hyperextended and prone to serious injury. An impact or unusual movement such as a quick twist or even jumping could accelerate the injury. The opposing muscle groups must be worked to ensure equal tension and strength in all the supporting tendons and muscles of the joint.

Figure W-15. - Wrist Curl Palms Down Dumbbell - Barbell - 3x8

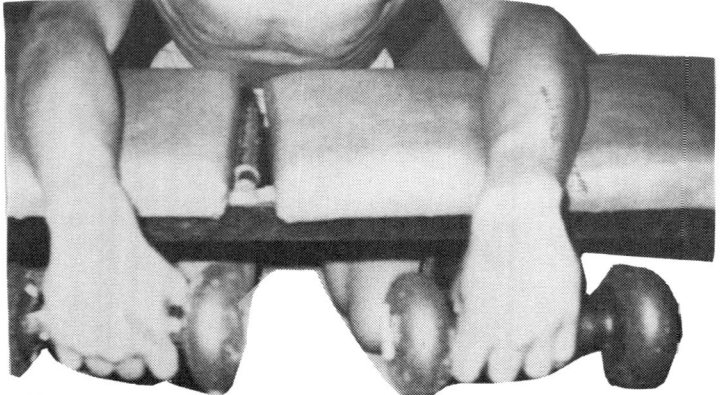

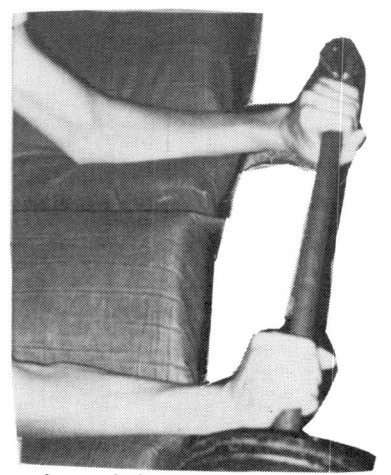

Begin - Dumbbell   Finish - Barbell

We have worked the flexor muscles of the arm (inside of lower arm) and the wrist in the palms up exercise on the last exercise day. Now we are going to work the extensor muscles and tendons of the back part of the lower arm and wrist.

As the picture shows, you can place the arm just above the wrist on your knees or on the edge of the bench and lower the hands up and down moving only the wrist joint. The arms should remain immobile, the elbows resting on the leg or the bench. The palms are facing the floor as they move up and down holding a weight that allows for full movement of the wrist joint. You will feel a tightness that will cease quickly when you stretch the muscle by moving the hand up and down without the weight. Do three sets of eight repetitions.

Figure W-16. - Trunk Twist Seated Trunk Twist - 3x10
Suspended Trunk Twist - 3x10

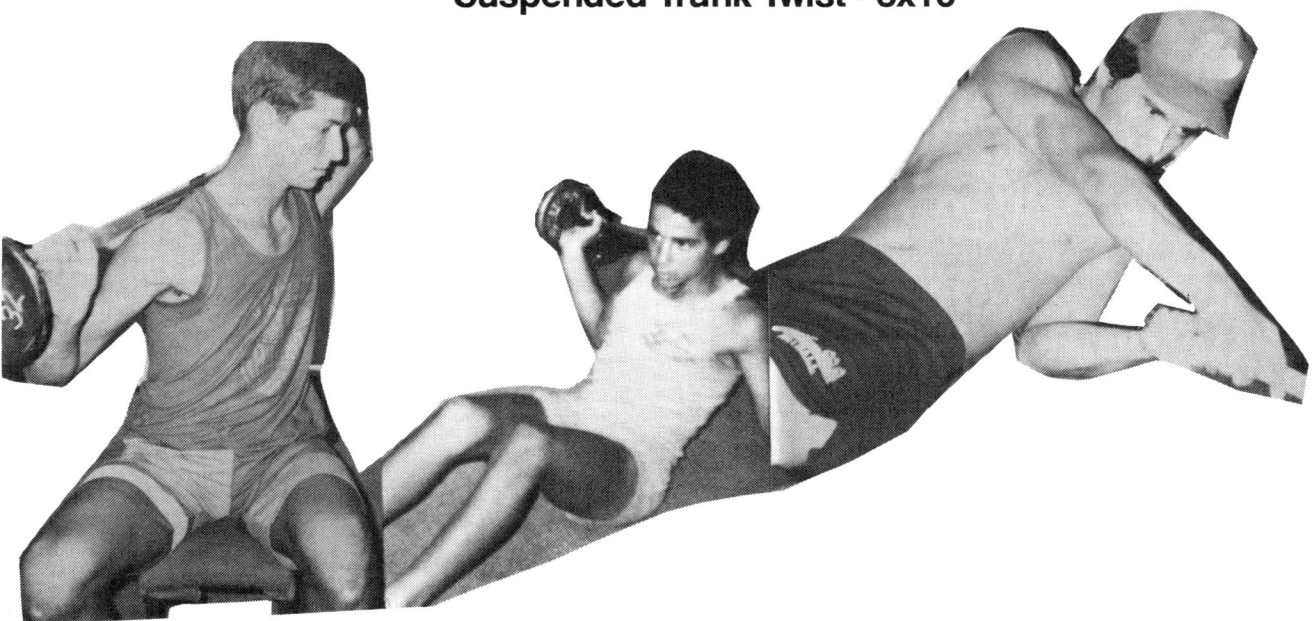

Beginner Trunk
Twist on bench with
barbell on shoulder

Slant Trunk Twist
Lean back on floor
(Intermediate level)

Trunk Twist
on Roman chair
for advanced

The beginner should begin this exercise seated on a flat bench with a barbell across the shoulders. The trainee will then twist from side to side allowing the abdominal muscles to stretch along with the spinae erectors (muscles to the sides of the back). This will build the strength necessary to perform the advanced exercise called the Suspended Trunk Twist. If the trainee does not have access to a roman chair for the Suspended Trunk Twist, he/she may use a couch or coffee table or the help of a spotter holding the legs down while the twist is executed.

The next step for the beginner is the Seated Lean Back Trunk Twist. The trainee sits on the floor with his/her feet held down by a spotter, or placed under a couch or chair while leaning back and twisting from side to side. At first the arms are held crossed at the chest and as ability and strength increase, the arms are held straight out and together from the chest while the trunk is twisted from side to side. The trainee will be amazed at the added resistance from this simple movement of the arms.

The advanced trainee will be able to lean back on the roman chair (can also be done on bleachers at school) and perform the Trunk Twist. When the advanced trainee develops strength in the torso area, he/she will be able to hold both arms straight out, above the chest, and move in a twisting movement with shoulders and trunk. After a few weeks of using the arms as weight, the advanced trainee can add additional weight carefully.

In the picture of the Twist on the roman chair, the trainee is using a dumbbell bar weighing three pounds. Notice the grip the youth is using on the bar. The grip is almost the same as that used in holding the bat or hockey stick.

You will feel the strength throughout the entire torso area and back. These are the muscles you use in throwing and hitting the baseball. I urge all readers to engage in this exercise only as your ability dictates. Use the three levels of ability as pictured and do not advance to the next level until you are capable of three sets of ten complete repetitions and do not feel overly exhausted.

Insert Figure W-17. - Supported Dumbbell Rowing (With Wrist Twist) - 3x8

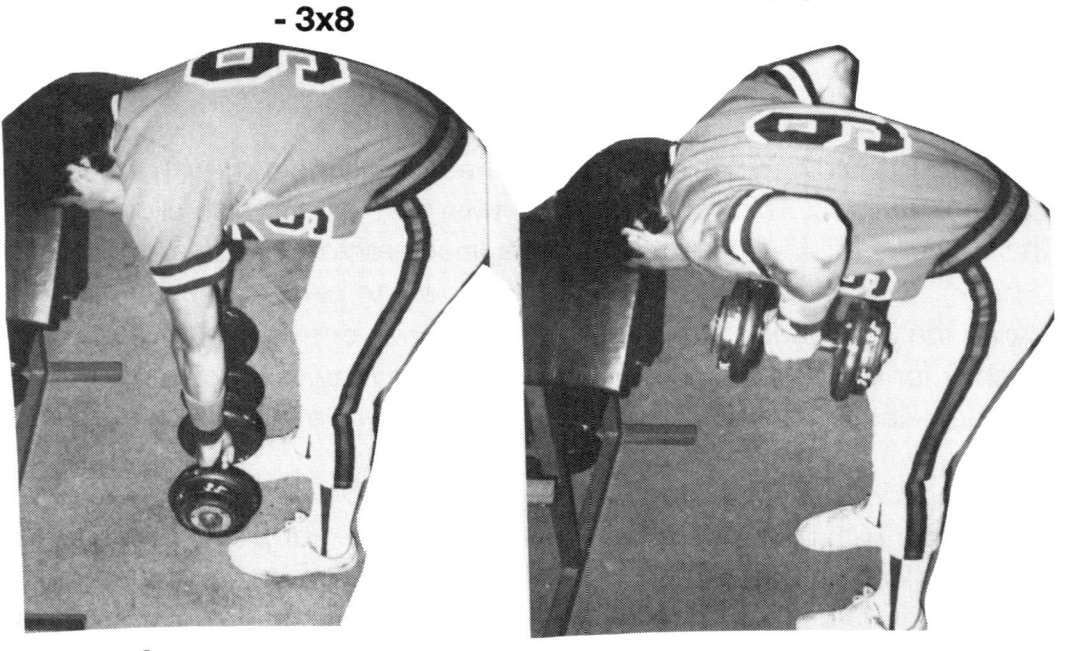

Start   Finish

The beginner should become accustomed to the movement and feel of this exercise before getting involved with unsupported rowing. We are using head support to ensure the back is not injured while performing the exercise. Later, as the trainee advances, he/she may try bent-over rowing with no support. You may also use barbells, as you become more proficient, to add variety to this workout.

You will feel the latissimus dorsi (major back muscle) stretch as you allow the weight to go all the way down. When you feel the stretch, begin to pull the weight up to the lower chest area. The movement should be done with a weight that would allow three sets of eight to be completed without overstraining. The weight must be controlled in the down motion so as to prevent a jerking of the elbow joint (epiphysis). Your head should be placed on an edge of a bench or back of a padded chair so that your back is at about 90 degrees. This exercise really helps to obtain the "V" shape while offering the building of power in the back for throwing and batting.

Figure W-18. - Seated Dumbbell Press - 3x10

Begin   End

In the last workout day we did a standing press while doing a squat. Figure W-6. Today we are going to perform the press while seated on the edge of a bench.

It is important that you permit the dumbbells to come down until your elbows almost touch your sides before raising them up over your head — without allowing the elbows to jerk upon reaching the point over your head.

Do not completely straighten your elbows at the top point. Keep the elbows slightly bent and then bring the weights down in a controlled fashion.

We use the dumbbells because they allow for a fuller movement of the muscles being worked. If you were to use a barbell, the movement would be hampered by the bar coming into contact with the chest (to the front press) or the back (to the rear press). We can utilize more muscles by using the dumbbells and also save time in the workout room.

If the trainee wishes to utilize more of the total arm in the exercise, he/she may begin the movement with the palms facing each other at the down position and then rotate the palms to face out as they rise to the overhead position. As the arms begin their descent, the palms will rotate to face each other at the down position. Repeat the movement the required sets and reps. The trainee will realize an almost automatic timing developing as the exercise is perfected. Note the similarity to the throwing movement of the arm.

Figure W-19. Alternate Arm Curl on Slant Bench (With Wrist Rotation) - 3x10 Each Arm

Alternate Arm Curl - Slant Bench

This exercise can work the deltoid muscles (shoulder), pectoralis minor (upper chest), biceps (upper arm), and lower arm, including the wrist. The head must be back on the slanted bench while holding the dumbbells down at each side of the bench.

Bring the right arm up rotating the wrist so the palm faces forward as you pass the hip area. The right arm comes to the anterior deltoid area (front shoulder) with the palm facing the shoulder.

When the right arm reaches the shoulder, the left arm begins the same movement upward as did the right arm. While the right arm begins its controlled downward movement, the left arm is rotating the palm forward at the hip to complete the movement at the left shoulder. The right arm will move down and rotate the palm toward the right side of the body as it passes the hip area.

When the athlete becomes coordinated and can benefit from the exercise without undue stress, he can raise the elbows when the arms reach the shoulder area. This added movement will tax the deltoids and minor pectoralis even more without additional weight.

Do not allow the weights to fall to the sides or fly outward from the body on the upward movement. You should feel the majority of the work in your biceps. Keep the dumbbells in control during all phases of the movement. This allows for equal development of strength and coordination in both arms and wrist.

Figure W-20. - Jump Rope - Forward - Backward - Crosswise - 100
(See as described in Figure W-10)

If you feel ready for advanced rope jumping and are able to perform backward and forward, try crossing the arms as pictured. Begin with both feet at once and progress to alternate feet.

This concludes the workout for this day (DAY TWO). Take a day of rest and then proceed to workout DAY THREE.

WORKOUT DAY THREE

To the instructor/coach

The third-day program places emphasis on the deltoids (shoulders) and upper body strength and endurance. If the trainee is not able to complete the sets and reps as instructed, please do not attempt to force completion. Allow the trainee to accomplish what he/she can do at their own pace until strength and agility have improved. I keep re-stating this throughout because overtraining can be devastating to the young athletes and turn them off weight training altogether.

Please consider the age, ability, and interest of your young athletes while training them. Allow the youngsters to modify the workouts as they feel comfortable as long as they are improving their athletic ability.

The young athlete will feel the strength and endurance building up in his upper body several hours after completion of this workout day. The power and strength will pay off in the throw and batting (if the trainee can hit the ball).

To the young athlete

After this day's workout you will not do weight training for forty-eight hours (two days of rest). This will allow the muscles to recuperate and to regain their strength. Remember, muscles need rest to gain in strength and power. You may use your days off for swimming, bicycling or any recreational activity you enjoy. The recreational activity will allow for a psychological recovery also.

Please remember these workouts are for improvements in strength, speed, endurance, and agility. They are not for body building or weight lifting. Nevertheless, you will notice a marked improvement in your physique with a total body and mind feeling of healthy energy.

Figure W-21. - Barbell Bench Press - 3x10

Start					End

You will find that using the barbell does not allow for the free movement as did the Dumbbell Bench Press. The barbell will be stopped at the chest. Do not allow the barbell to touch the chest.

When the barbell is permitted to bounce off the chest, the chest pushes the rib cage out, which causes the backbone (vertebrae) attached to the ribs to move outward causing a pain which the trainee (or inexperienced instructor) is unable to understand.

I teach my athletes not to touch the chest so they will be accustomed to the feeling of a completed bench press without causing harm to the rib cage, sternum (mid portion of the bottom of the chest usually hit) and vertebrae (backbone). My trainees are permitted to lower the barbell to the chest within the thickness of their finger. Once they become used to this movement and the stop point, they do not suffer the injuries mentioned.

If you go to most gyms or high schools, you will see the young athletes pounding the barbell off their chest while arching their back and forcing a weight through the repetitions. This is a waste of time and only causes harm. The forced movement has no benefit to the body and causes harm to the lumbar (lower back) region by compressing them harshly.

The National Strength and Conditioning Association has an excellent article with drawings on this subject of bench pressing correctly. I urge any interested instructor, coach, or parent, to write to the Association and ask for a copy of "An In Depth Analysis of the Bench Press." It appeared in the October-November 1982 issue of the "NSCA Journal."

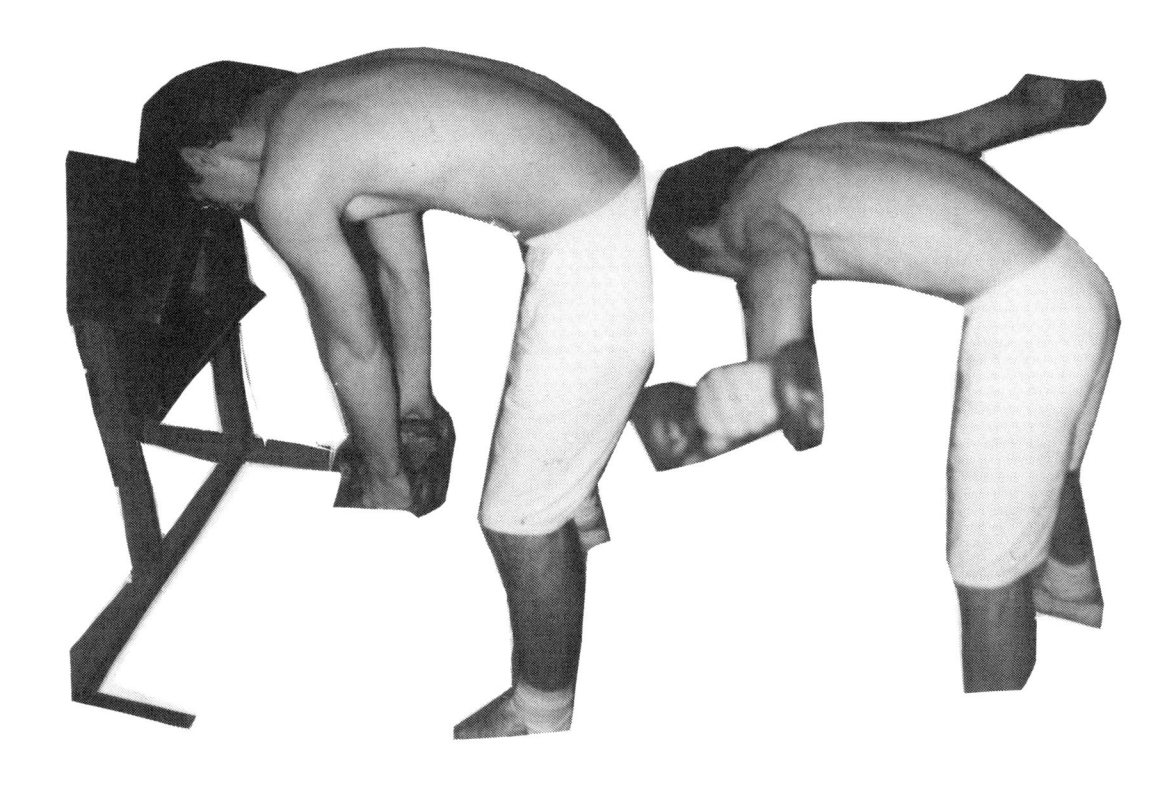

Figure W-22. - Supported Dumbbell Bent Over Side Raises - 3x8

Start   Finish

Use an edge of a high bench or back of a chair, or padded barbell placed upon the uprights for this exercise. We used this method of support in exercise W-17, (the Supported Dumbbell Rowing)

In the Bent Over Side Raise (supported) With Dumbbells we work the rear deltoids (back of shoulder), anterior deltoids (front shoulder), trapezius (neck muscle), and the latissimus dorsi (major back muscle). The pectoralis major (chest muscle) is worked to some degree on the down motion of the dumbbells. The greatest emphasis is placed on the rear deltoids which strengthens the muscles supporting the rotator cuff to the body.

Supporting the head allows concentration of effort to the deltoids without causing strain to the back (lumbar region). It is important that the dumbbells be raised just over the height of the shoulders and straight out from the shoulders.

The weights should be raised without excess speed and returned to the starting point with control. They should not be permitted to just "fall" down to the starting point. Rest twenty seconds between each repetition. The weight should not be too heavy, preventing full upward movement and controlled movement downward.

Figure W-23. - Seated Side Raises with Wrist Rotation - 3x10

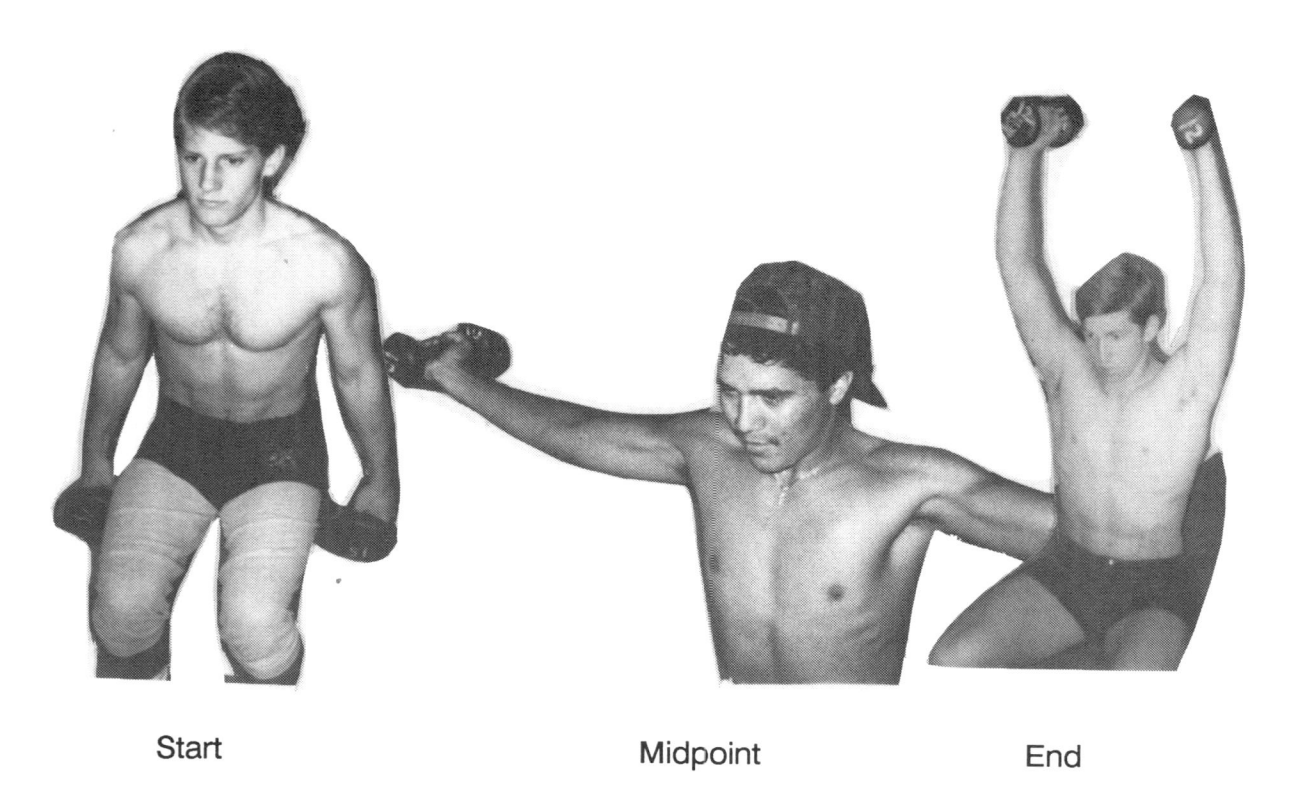

Start   Midpoint   End

This exercise is a flexor movement, which is the opposite of the last exercise, which is an extensor exercise. They are opposite muscles controlling the shoulder area from a different angle. We are using different angles to strengthen all parts of the shoulder and upper back. We do this to prevent one part of the muscle group becoming too strong and pulling a part of the body out of line. Many athletes do not realize that all opposing muscle groups must be worked equally to prevent pain and strains from occurring in a muscle that is not receiving enough training or a muscle that is favored over another and is trained to excess.

To do the Seated Side Raise With Wrist Rotation, sit on the edge of the bench and raise the dumbbells with the palms facing the floor until you reach your shoulders. When you have reached your shoulder height, without stopping, turn your palms up and continue the raise to the overhead position with the palms still facing each other.

On the downward movement, you have the palms up until you reach the shoulder height and then you turn the palms toward the floor until the dumbbells reach the bottom point. Repeat for three sets of ten repetitions with the weights in control. If the exercise cannot be done 3x10 with a lighter weight, then do fewer repetitions until strength is built up.

Figure W-24.- Slant Bench Massive Chest Expander - Dumbbell-3x10

Begin and End   Midpoint Expansion Forward   Arms and Chest Fully Spread

The chest expansion requires work by many muscles, though the pectoralis major (the massive chest muscle), will do most of the work during the circular movement of the dumbbells. The dumbbells must be light enough for the trainee to hold straight as in the midpoint picture. The arms begin close to the side, and the dumbbells are moved straight out, to the front, with the elbows slightly bent. The dumbbells should be on the same level as the lower part of the chest and the dumbbells are spread apart and then circled back to the beginning position. Each arm makes a small circle as the arms are brought together at the chest, then circled apart, and then circled back together again.

You will feel the deltoids (shoulders), latissimus dorsi (back), and forearm, including wrist, working as you do this exercise. Be sure the dumbbells are not too heavy so you can complete the entire movement without overtiring or straining yourself.

Figure W-25. Standing Calf Raise - 2x16.

See the written description in W-4 for an explanation and picture of this exercise. Remember, do the raises light and fast for baseball (and track and other quick running sports).

Figure W-26. - Upright Rowing - 3x10 (Barbell)

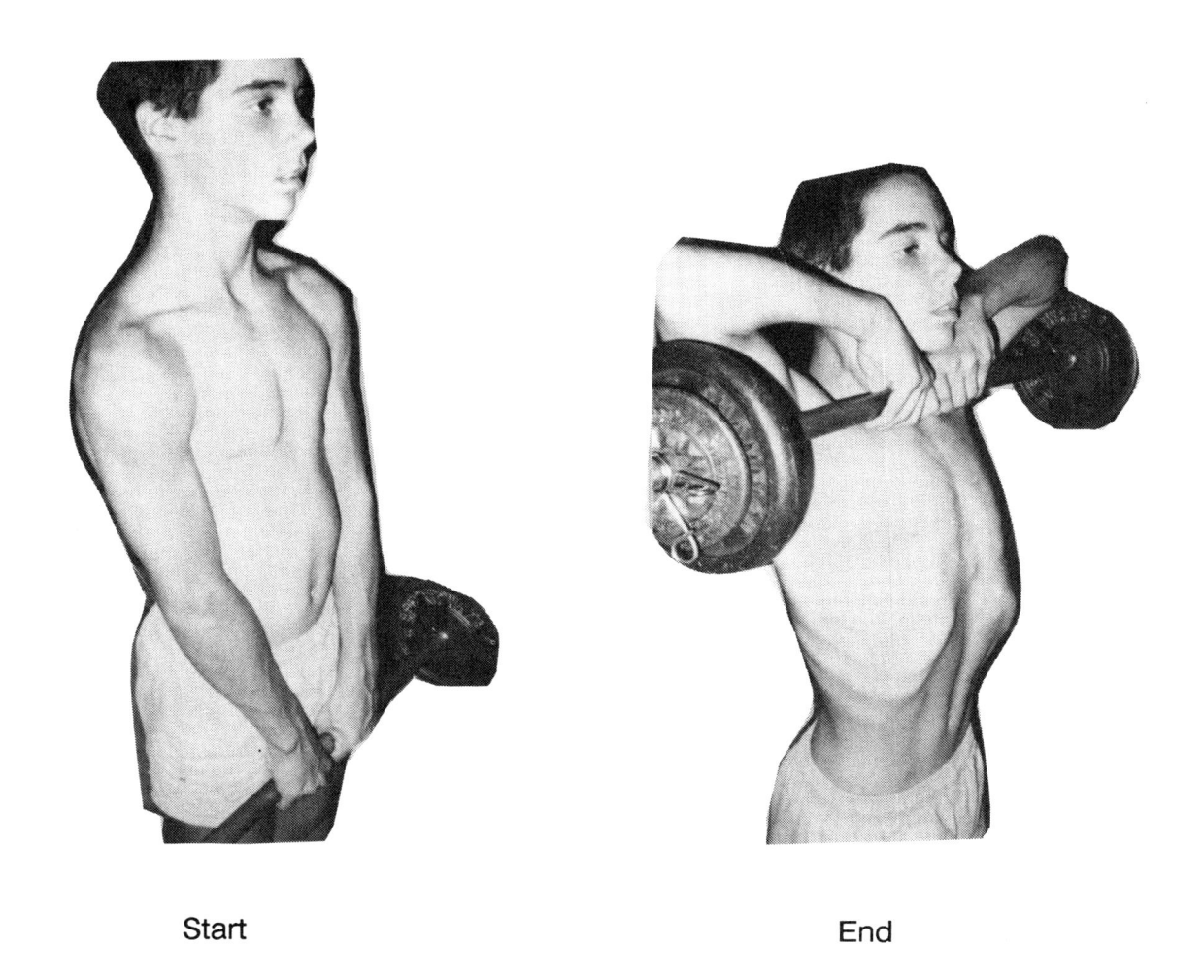

Start   End

Upright Rowing is a very exhilarating exercise. The movement forces the chest to expand while working the smaller upper muscles of the back (rhomboid and scapular areas). You will feel the larger muscles of the back working also (latissimus dorsi and spinae flexors). The stomach will work also in the external obliques (along the side of the stomach in the frontal area). The neck muscles (trapezius) will also be worked.

Begin by standing with your hands about one inch apart on the barbell. Bring the weight up to the point just under your chin, which is lifted up. Focus your eyes on the ceiling above you. As you bring the weight up to your uplifted chin, your elbows will automatically spread out and cause your chest to spread also.

You should breathe in (inhale) deeply as the pull is progressing upward until the barbell reaches the high point along with the completion of the inhale.

Do not allow the barbell to fall to the starting point. Do not jerk the weight, but keep the movements smooth, and you will reap the benefits of this exhilarating exercise.

There is an interesting side note. If you want some anterior deltoid (front shoulder) work, spread your hands shoulder width apart on the bar and you will feel the work shift to those areas. You can see how important proper instruction is for full athletic development in all body parts. Do three sets of ten if you can.

Figure W-27. - Reverse Dumbbell - Barbell Curl (with High Rise) - 3x10

Start
Barbell

End
Barbell

High Rise
Barbell

Trainees are slow to appreciate this exercise, but are quick to admit they feel the strength developing in areas they never felt before. When done correctly, this exercise will work the triceps (upper back of arm) and lower top side of the forearm) extensor carpi radialis longus). The trainees are surprised to feel the muscles working in the back, upper chest, shoulders, and neck muscles.

If the trainee is permitted to throw the barbell (or dumbbells) up to the chest, the muscles are not worked properly and they will not develop properly. The trainee must keep the torso straight, move only the arms to the chest area, and control the downward movement until the arms are just slightly bent at the elbow.

Do three sets of ten if you can. Once you master the ability to do three sets of ten properly without strain you can try a more advanced movement. Instead of adding more weight, you raise your elbows while tilting your upper body back slightly to allow the deltoids to feel the work also. You can see this in the third picture of Figure W-27.

Figure W-28. Jump Rope 100 repetitions forward-beginner-100 forward then 100 backward for experienced trainees.

This concludes the weight training portion of this book. I will now discuss other exercises the trainee can perform for therapy after an injury or to prevent injury.

CHAPTER XVII

ARM THERAPY EXERCISES USED BY SPORTS CLINICS AND TRAINEES

This section will discuss various exercises used to perform therapy on the arm. Skelton's technique was provided to the author by John C. Lincoln Hospital's Sports Medicine Clinic in Phoenix, Arizona. I have used this therapy on young ballplayers and have found it to be very effective.

The pictures are self-explanatory. Please make sure the weight is "therapeutic." It should be enough to offer resistance without causing strain. The trainee should feel the muscle working without pain. At the point where pain is felt, the movement should stop. You will find that movement will increase as the muscles are therapeutically worked over a week's time.

If there are tendons or ligaments torn, this therapy will not help until healing has occurred by surgery, or a doctor has prescribed rest to allow minor tears to heal before therapy begins. This therapy works well with slight strains. It strengthens the surrounding muscle fibers to affect the pulling of the stronger, less damaged, muscles.

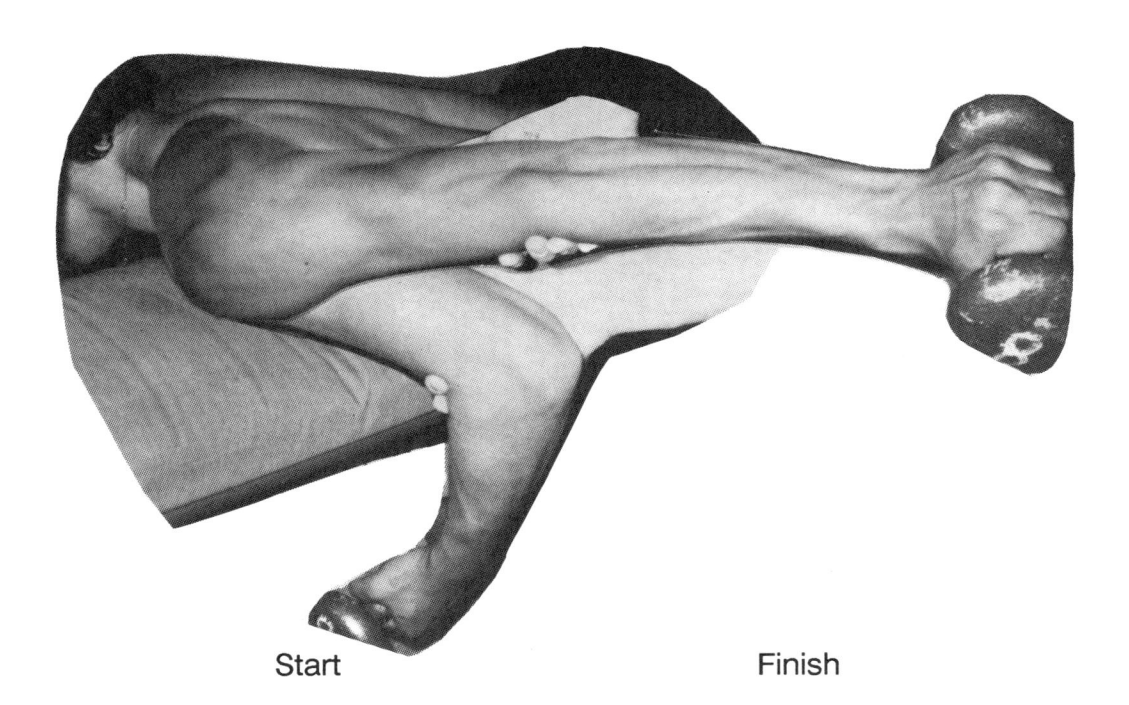

Figure T-1 - Skelton's Technique for Arm Therapy - 2x12

Start   Finish

Figure T-1 shows Bobby with a helper holding his arm for added support and strictness of movement. You see the deltoids and extensors of the lower arm working as well as the triceps of the upper arm. Also notice the extensors of the wrist.

The National Strength and Conditioning Association carried a series of shoulder/arm strengthening exercises in its Journal, April/May 1981. I have used this therapy, too, and found that the trainees responded very well.

Figure T-2 - Bench Shoulder Rotator Curl Barbell or Dumbbell

Start   Finish

Figure T-2 illustrates the rotator curl on the T-Bench. The dumbbells allow more downward movement while the barbell inhibits movement to the sides.

Notice Bobby keeps his elbows on the bench to isolate the work to the rotator cuff. In both Figures T-1 and T-2, you can see work in the flexor and extensor muscles of the forearm as well as the epiphysis (elbow). Bobby brings his arms as far back as possible without causing strain in the areas to be worked. He then comes an equal distance forward until the movement is completed. Try two sets of twelve repetitions with a very light weight for each of these exercises until strength is returned to the area.

In the rotator shoulder curl, you are strengthening the deltoids at the fibers which hold the rotator cuff in place. The therapeutic value of this movement is that the motion forces the deltoids to strengthen in areas seldom worked in other training exercises. It will offer relief for slight muscle strains. Should pain occur, the movement should be stopped at that point and gradual movement introduced. This exercise will help relieve the pain sometimes felt in the front shoulder (anterior deltoid) after throwing. Remember to stretch before doing these exercises.

CHEAP TRAINING AND THERAPY AIDS

I have found one of the greatest and cheapest training aids available to the young ballplayer. Your investment would be about 79 cents. All you need is some string and a plastic Wiffle golf ball and a broomstick.

Figure T-3 - Batting String and Whiffle Ball develop eye-hand coordination. Used by many professional ball players in their formative years.

The Whiffle ball in the photo has been darkened to illustrate the simplicity of the training aid.

Notice Bobby is using the entire body to address the ball. His motion will mimic the "game" situation which will aid in the mental attitude. Peripheral vision is enhanced by the natural return action of the ball.

The trainee is to hit the Wiffle golf ball when it is returning toward him after the initial hit. The returning ball will mimic a pitched ball in the returning swing. The Wiffle ball's path will be unpredictable as would be that of a pitched ball.

The slender broomstick forces the child to develop eye-hand coordination while having fun. My trainees will perform this exercise while waiting for their parents to pick them up after a workout; or they will make time for the special training on the "batting string." It is something they can do without much supervision.

If the trainee has been injured and recovery of strength without pain is sufficient, the aids can be used for therapeutic purposes.

If pain persists, movement must be stopped. The range of motion may be increased as healing progresses. The increase in flexibility would be a subjective method to gauge strength and range of motion increases in each quadrant discussed in this chapter.

Another training aid I have used in working the wrist and rotator cuff is bicycle inner tubes. They are cut into strips and one end is tied to a stationary object. The free end is attached to a rubber coated baseball. A hole is drilled through the baseball and a strong wire looped around the inner tube and tied to the other end of the ball.

Figure T-4 - Cheap Training Aids - Rotator Cuff - 50 each arm

Begin (Top)   End

The trainee can hold the ball at his side and do various wrist exercises up and down and to the sides to develop grip and strength.

The rotator cuff can be worked by making circles as though in the throwing motion. The movements are slow and not hurried. Movement in the muscle should be fluid with no strain in any quadrant. I urge trainees to work both arms so that symmetry of body parts in appearance and strength can be maintained.

If old bicycle inner tubes cannot be found, you may wish to use strands of surgical tubing. Please be aware that all rubber products will dry out and become worn. Do not use an old dried-out piece of rubber that may break and snap at you during the stretch.

Figures T-5a b, c, and d illustrate movements using the inner tube training aid. Notice the wrist action in all possible natural movements involving throwing. The wrist should be permitted to move in the full range to exercise wrist and arm flexor/extensors. Do at least 35 of each direction.

Figures T-5a. - Fourth Quadrant Movement of Wrist and Rotator Cup
Figure T-5b. - Extensor Flexor
Figure T-5c. - Wrist Pronator-Adduction (Top Right of Page)
Figure T-5d. - Abductor Movement (Bottom)

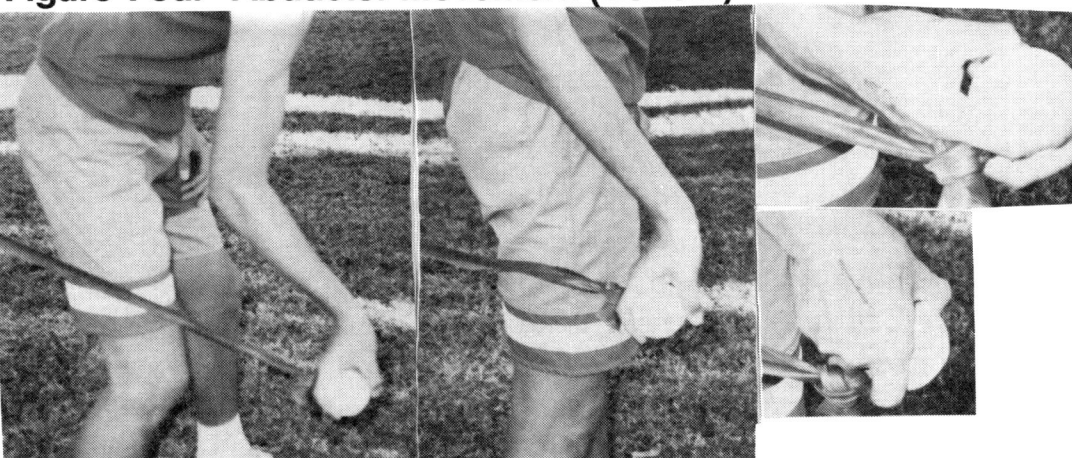

Fig. T-5a. Fourth Quadrant Movement of Wrist and Rotator Cuff.

Fig. T-5b. Wrist Extensor Flexor

Fig T-5c. (Top) Wrist Pronator-Adduction
Fig. T-5d. (Below) Abductor Movement

Figure T-5a shows the fourth quadrant position of the rotator cuff training. Notice the wrist work necessary to complete a circle. T-5b displays flexor/extensor movement of the wrist with an inner tube. Figure T-5c shows pronation of adductors at the wrist. Figure T-5c shows the abductor longus (lateral wrist muscle) raised and lowered. Notice the grip on the ball and the movement with the palm facing the body. The wrist (and grip) is further strengthened by exercises as shown in the weight training section of this book displaying wrist curls and arm curls. The inner tube aids are to provide an in-season, or to enhance a pre-season, program for wrist, arm, and shoulder strength and conditioning.

Figure T-6 - Little League Elbow and Wrist Strengthening Therapy with Light Dumbbell - Wrist Up - Wrist Down - Do 3x8 or 3x12 in Season

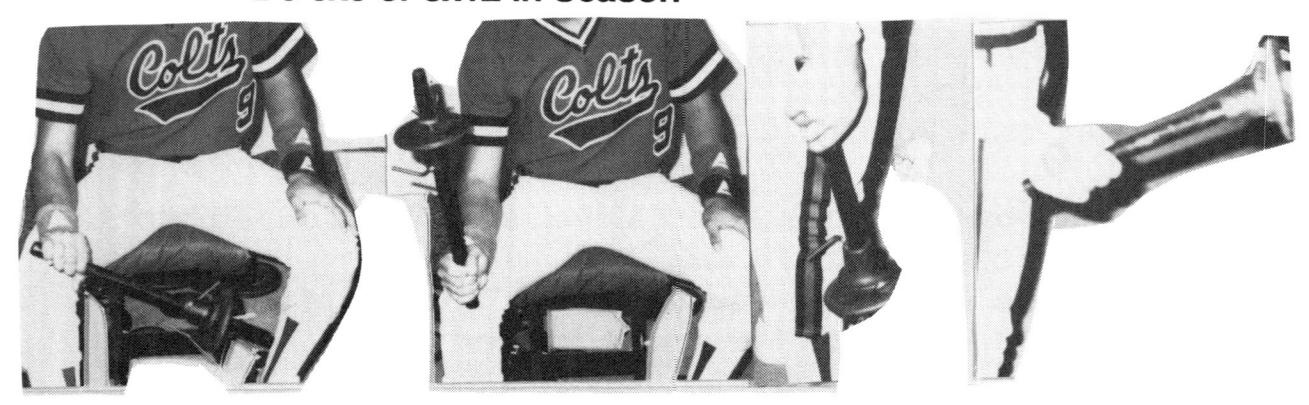

| Sitting Knee Support Begin | Sitting Knee Support End | Standing Begin | Standing - End |

Figure T-6 shows another method of therapy for Little League elbow. Light weight is placed at the end of a dumbbell bar and the motion is up and down. First, palms are gripping the bar with the palms up, After eight to twelve reps, the dumbbell is placed in the other hand to keep the body's development symmetrical. After the reps in the working hand are completed, the bar is placed in the resting hand with the palms down, and the reps are completed as before. I have my trainees do this with both wrists so that equal development is enhanced. Don't forget, the entire body is involved in throwing a ball (as well as hitting it).

The trainee may do this standing or sitting, with the arm supported on the edge of the knee if sitting, or the edge of a bench if standing or sitting. The wrist curl, as discussed in Chapter XVI, is also a method of wrist strengthening.

Figure T-7 - Little League Elbow Strengthening Therapy with Palms Facing the Body and the Wrist moving Up and Down (Pronating - Extending) - 2x12 Each Wrist

Begin   End

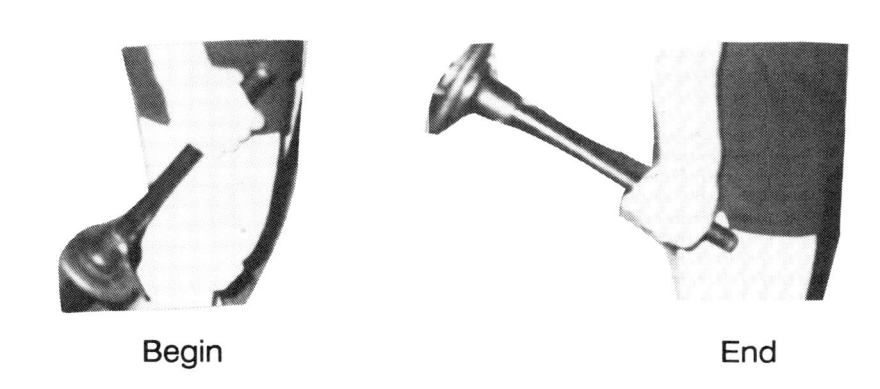

Figure T-7 shows the wrist working the abductors more intensely. The movement of the exercises as discussed from Figures T-6 and T-7 allows the athlete to work most of the tendons of the wrist extensors, pronators and abductors. The smaller tendons near the end of the wrist (carpi extensors/flexors) can be damaged severely if the trainee attempts too much weight during this therapy. All areas are to be worked equally to prevent one set of tendons causing stress on the opposing tendons due to overtraining in one quadrant only.

Workout Sheet For Program Two - Day One
Baseball

Trainees are advised to familiarize themselves with Maitland's book, "Beginning Weight Training For Young Athletes" (published in 1986) before starting this special program for the baseball player. Weight Training Days are alternated, i.e. Monday, Wednesday, Friday, with the weekends for recreation and Plyometric Training. Trainees should modify the workouts according to in-season/off-season schedules and consider the sport for which weight training is to be used. If injury occurs cease training and consult a sports medicine specialist. Heavier, demanding schedules are for Off-season, otherwise use the noted "sets" and "reps". Breathe properly in all exercises. "Reps" may be higher or lower but not more than 16 nor less than 8. Read text for reason of sets and reps. Modify as condition improves.
—EXERCISE—

Warm Up and Stretch Before Workouts!!!

Read text for reason of sets and reps. Modify as condition improves. —EXERCISE—	Pre-season Poundage 1st month light/high reps	Medium weight Poundage 2nd month in season	Off season more Poundage lower reps 3rd month	Poundage condition advanced
W1 Flat dumbbell bench press 3x10				
W2 Clean to shoulders 3x10				
W3 Shoulder Shrug 3x10 dumbbell or barbell				
W4 Standing Calf raise 2x16, 3x10 or 3x12				
W5 Torso Circle 2x16 each direction				
W6 Standing dumbbell press squat 2x16				
W7 Strict arm curl 3x8 dumbbell or barbell				
W8 Tricep extension 3x8 dumbbell or barbell				
W9 Wrist curl palms up 3x10				
W10 Jump rope 100 forward & backward alt. feet				

© 1988 by William J. Maitland. Blank spaces are trainees/coaches modification as conditioning allows.

Workout Sheet For Program Two - Day Two
Baseball

Trainees are advised to familiarize themselves with Maitland's book, "Beginning Weight Training For Young Athletes" (published in 1986) before starting this special program for the baseball player. Weight Training Days are alternated, i.e. Monday, Wednesday, Friday, with the weekends for recreation and Plyometric Training. Trainees should modify the workouts according to in-season/off-season schedules and consider the sport for which weight training is to be used. If injury occurs cease training and consult a sports medicine specialist. Heavier, demanding schedules are for Off-season, otherwise use the noted "sets" and "reps". Breathe properly in all exercises. "Reps" may be higher or lower but not more than 16 nor less than 8.

Warm Up and Stretch before Workouts!!!				
Read text for reason of sets and reps. Modify as condition improves. —EXERCISE—	Pre-season Poundage 1st month light/high reps	Medium weight Poundage 2nd month in season	Off season more poundage lower reps. 3rd month	Poundage condition advanced
W11 Slant Dumbbell bench press 3x10				
W12 Sprint Machine or Lungs @ weights 3x10				
W13 Thigh Curls/ machine or leg weights 3x8				
W14 Leg extensions/ Mach or weights 3x8/3x10				
W15 Wrist Curl/palms down 3x12/3x8				
W16 Seated Trunk twist or Roman chair 3x10				
W17 Supported Dumbbell Rowing 3x8/3x10				
W18 Seated Dumbbell Press/twist 3x10				
W19 Alternate Arm curls slant bench 3x10				
W20 Jump rope/ alternate feet/100 forward & backward alt. feet				

© 1988 by William J. Maitland. Blank spaces are trainees/coaches modification as conditioning allows.

Workout Sheet For Program Two - Day Three
Baseball

Students are advised to familiarize themselves with Maitland's book, "Beginning Weight Training For Young Athletes" (published in 1986) before starting this special program for the baseball player. Weight Training Days are alternated, i.e. Monday, Wednesday, Friday, with the weekends for recreation and Plyometric Training. Trainees should modify the workouts according to in-season/off-season schedules and consider the sport for which weight training is to be used. If injury occurs cease training and consult a sports medicine specialist. Heavier, demanding schedules are for Off-season, otherwise use the noted "sets" and "reps". Breathe properly in all exercises. "Reps" may be higher or lower but not more than 16 nor less than 8.

Warm Up and Stretch before Workouts!!!

Read text for reason of sets and reps. Modify as condition improves. —EXERCISE—	Pre-season Poundage 1st month light/high reps		Medium weight Poundage 2nd month in season		Off season more poundage lower reps. 3rd month		Poundage condition advanced	
W21 Flat barbell bench press 3x10/3x8								
W22 Supported Bent Over side raise/ dumbbell 3x8								
W23 Seated side (rotator) arm raise 3x10/3x8								
W24 Slant bench massive chest expander 3x10								
W25 Standing calf raise 3x12/3x16								
W26 Upright Rowing (Barbell) 3x12/2x16								
W27 Reverse curls 3X10/3x8								
W28 Jump Rope 100 Forward 100 backward if able								

© 1988 by William J. Maitland
Blank spaces are trainees/coaches modification as conditioning allows.

About the Author

The author, William J. "Bill" Maitland.

Bill Maitland has trained young athletes through adulthood for thirty years and continues to do so at his training facility in Phoenix, Arizona. Mr. Maitland has enjoyed coaching and playing sports all of his life and was an athletic director in Tucson, Arizona before moving to Phoenix. He began his coaching training career with the East End YMCA in Painesville, Ohio, at the age of 17. He was the highest paid riding master in the State of Ohio.

Mr. Maitland received his college education at Kent State University (Ohio) where he did graduate level independent study of "Psychology and the Athlete". After leaving Kent State he completed his studies at the Uiversity of Arizona.

The author's first book for athletes, *BEGINNING WEIGHT TRAINING FOR YOUNG ATHLETES, —AGES 12 thru ADULT,* has sold worldwide and has enjoyed excellent reviews from its readers. *WEIGHT TRAINING FOR GIFTED ATHLETES— AGES 14 through ADULTS* is the advanced program. The book follows the graduates of the first program throughout their adolescent and adult training.

Maitland's training books are endorsed by Dr. Art Mollen-founder of the Phoenix 10-K Run and newspaper columnist of health and sports issues in athletic and recreational training. He also heads the "SOUTHWEST HEALTH INSTITUTE" in Phoenix, Scottsdale and Sun City, Arizona.

COACH MAITLAND HAS BEEN A MEMBER OF THE NATIONAL STRENGTH AND CONDITIONING ASSOCIATION SINCE 1981.

BIBLIOGRAPHY

Anderson, Bob. *Stretching.* Shelter Publications, Bolinas, California, 1980.

Cimino, John S. (Department of Physical Education, Oregon State University). *A One Year Periodization Conditioning Program Specific to Fastball Pitches.* National Strength & Conditioning Association Journal, Vol. 9, No. 2 (April-May) 1987.

Croce, Pat. *The Baseball Player's Guide to Sports Medicine.* Leisure Press, Human Kinetics Publishers, Champaign, Illinois, 1987.

DeRenne, Coop, Ph.D. (University of Hawaii, Honolulu). *Physical Demands and Biochemical Basis for Baseball Conditioning.* National Strength & Conditioning Association Journal, Vol. 12, No. 4 (August-September) 1990.

The Donut: Does It Improve Bat Velocity. National Strength & Conditioning Association Journal, Vol. 13, No. 3, 1991.

Einstein, Charles. *How to Coach, Manage, and Play Little League Baseball.* Simon and Schuster, New York, 1968.

Feldman, Jay. *Straight Talk About the Curbe Ball.* American Health, October 1984.

Ford, Whitey, with Phil Pepe. *Slick: My Life In and Around Baseball.* Dell, New York. 1987.

Garhammer, John, Ph.D. (Director, International Maxachievement Institutes). *A Kinesiological Analysis Of Hitting For Baseball.* National Strength & Conditioning Association Journal, (April-May)) 1983.

Hodges, Gil, with Frank Slocum. *The Game Of Baseball.* Crown Publisher, Inc., New York. 1969.

Jackson, Reggie, with Joel Hl Cohen. *Inside Hitting.* Henry Regnery Company, Chicago. 1975.

Jacobs, Pat, C.S.C.S. (Associate Strength and Conditioning Coach, University of Miami, Coral Gables, Florida). *The Overhand Baseball Pitch: A Kinesiological Analysis and Related Strength-conditioning Programming.* National Strength & Conditioning Association Journal, Vol. 9, No. 1 (February-March) 1987.

Lefebvre, Jim. (Batting and Conditioning Coach, San Francisco Giants). *Hitting the Baseball; Let's Understand the Process.* National Strength & Conditioning Association Journal. April-May 1983.

Mitchelli, Lyle J., M.D. (Director, Division of Sports Medicine, Boston Children's Hospital). *Physiological and Orthopedic Considerations for Strengthening the Pre-Pubescent Athlete*. National Strength & Conditioning Association Journal, Vol. 7, No. 6, 1985.

Seaver, Tom *The Art of Pitching*. Hearst Books, New York. 1984.

Southmayd, William, M.D., and Marshall Hoffman. *Sports Health: The Complete Book of Athletic Injuries*. Quick Fox, New York. 1981.

Sutton, Don. *How to Throw a Curveball*. Follet Publishing, Chicago, 1977.

Maitland, William J., *Beginning Weight Training For Youth Athletes - Ages 12 thru Adult*. Maitland Enterprises Publishing, Phoenix, 1986.

Maitland, William J. *Weight Training for Gifted Athletes - ages 14 thru Adult*. Maitland Enterprises Publishing, Phoenix, 1990.

FURTHER READING AND RESEARCH SOURCES CONCERNING TRAINING AND CONDITIONING

Davis, Joel. *Endorphins-New Waves in Brain Chemistry*. Doubleday and Company. 1984.

Thommen, George, S. *Biorhythms-Is This Your Day?* Crown Publishers, 1973, Reprint 1987.

Fixx, James. *Masimum Sports Performance*. Random House, New York 1985.

Glasser; William M.D. *Take Effective Control Of Your Life*. Harper and Rowe, N.Y. 1984.

Diagram of Visual Information. 1980.

Gray Anatomy, Marshall Publishing, Inc. 1956.

The Parents' Book of Physical Fitness for Children From Infancy Through Adolescence. New York Antheneum, 1976.

The Columbia University Complete Home Medical Guide. Crown Publishers, 1985.

Dr. Lawrence Power, M.D. *The Power Plan For Health*. American Health Magazine, November 1986, vol. 5; No. 9.

Brody, Jane. *Jane Brody's Nutrition Book* and *Jane Brody's Good Food Book* (W.W. Norton).

O'Shea, Pat. Ed. D. Oregon State University and Pitreli, John, M.A., South Shore Sports Medicine, Bayshore, N.Y. Sports *Performance Series - Rope Jumping*, National Strength and Conditioning Association Journal; Vol. 8, No. 4, August-September, 1986.

Takano, Bob. *Coaching Optimal Techniques in The Snatch And Clean And Jerk*, National Strength and Conditioning Association Journal, October-November, 1987, Vol. 9, No. 5.

Algra, Bruce. *An In Depth Analysis Of The Bench Press*. National Strength And Conditioning Association, October-November 1982.

Elam, Reid, Strength Coach Oregon State University. *A Comparison of the Effects of Two Different Frequencies of Training on Neuromuscular Skill Development in Rope Jumping*. National Strength and Conditioning Association Journal, Vol. 3, No. 6, April-May 1982.

Grandjean, Ann C., R.D., M.S. and Schaefer, Arnold E., Ph.D., Associate Director and Director of the Swanson Center for Nutrition, Inc., Omaha, Nebraska. *Protein Need And Muscle Gain*. National Strength and Conditioning Association Journal, August-September 1982.

Hecker, Arthur L., Ph.D. and Wheeler, Keith B., Ph.D.,*Protein; A Misunderstood Nutrient For The Athlete*. National Strength and Conditioning Association Journal, Vol. 7, No. 6, 1985.

Wurtman, Judith, Ph.D., *Food For Thought (and Mood)*. New Age Journal, March-April 1987.

Pearson, David and Cotil, David. *Use Of Anabolic Steroids By National Level Athletes*. National Strength and Conditioning Association Journal, Vol. 3 No. 2, April-May 1981.

Lamberg, Lynne, *Dreams-Now You Can Make Them Work For You*. American Health Magazine, July 1987.

Carper, Jean. *Jean Carper's Complete Nutrition Guide*, Bantam Book, N.Y. New York, April 1987.

Troiano, Linda. *Hot Weather Downer-Cold Temperatures Can Lift Low Summer Spirits*. American Health Magazine, July-August, 1988.

Allman, William F. *How To Play It Cool*. Hippocrates Magazine, May-June 1988.

Chu, Donald A., R.PT., Ph.D., and Plummer, Lisa, M.S. *Jumping Into Plyometrics; The Language of Plyometrics*. National Strength and Conditioning Association Journal, Vol 6, No. 5, October-November, 1985.

Cornelius, William L., Ph.D. *Flexibility; Exercises Beneficial To The Hip Joint But Questionable For The Knee*. National Strength and Conditioning Association Journal, Vol. 6 No. 5 October-November 1984.

Kraemer, William J., Ph.D. *The Adolescent Athlete: The Challenge Of Training The Three Sport Athlete*. National Strength and Conditioning Association Journal Vol. 6, No. 5, October-November 1984.

Varona, Judy, Ph.D., *Research Application; Fitness In Prepubescent Children-Implications For Exercise Training*. National Strength and Conditioning Association Journal, Vol. 6, No. 6, November 6, 1985.

Bryan, Susan McKearney. *Kids and Sports - Is Sports Training Harming Our Children?* Vim and Vigor Magazine, Winter 1988.

Fike, Steven, T.D., Sport Nutritionist, Swanson Center For Nutrition, Omaha, Nebraska. *Toxicity of Vitamin Supplements*. National Strength and Conditioning Association Journal, Vol. 5, No. 5, 1987.

Fleck, Steven J., and Kraemer, William J. NSCA Research Committee: *The Overtraining Syndrome*. National Strength and Conditioning Association Journal, August-September 1982.

Garhammer; John, Ph.D., Biomechanics Laboratory Department of Kinesiology, UCLA, Los Angeles, Calif. Freeweight Equipment For The Development Of Athletic Strength and Power-Part I-Machine Vs. Freeweights. National Strength and Conditioning Association Journal, December-January 1982. Machine Vs. Freeweights Part II, NSCSA Journal February-March 1982.

HERE'S HOW YOU CAN ORDER BOOKS

SEND CHECK OR MONEY ORDER
IN U.S. FUNDS TO:

MAITLAND ENTERPRISES
PUBLISHING
8118 NORTH 28th. AVENUE
PHOENIX, ARIZONA 85051

PLEASE SEND_____ COPIES OF **BEGINNING WEIGHT TRAINING FOR YOUNG ATHLETES** (ages 12 thru adult) 8 1/2 x 11 — Paperback $9.95 each retail-post paid. ISBN#0-936-759-00-3.

PLEASE SEND_____ COPIES OF **WEIGHT TRAINING FOR GIFTED ATHLETE-AGES 14 THRU ADULT**. (ISBN#0-936-759-01-1) 8 1/2 x 11 — Paperback $17.95 retail-plus $2.00 postage/handling retail-U.S. Funds.

PLEASE ACCEPT MY ORDER FOR YOUR BOOK
YOUNG BALL PLAYERS GUIDE TO SAFE PITCHING (ages eight thru adult). $14.95
ISBN 0-936759-14-3

PLEASE SEND _____ COPIES WHEN THEY ARE AVAILABLE.

ENCLOSED FIND $_____ FOR PAYMENT OF BOOKS AS LISTED ABOVE. I UNDERSTAND THAT PRICES MAY CHANGE DUE TO MATERIAL AND LABOR OR OTHER UNFORESEEN INCREASES IN PRODUCTION COST WITHOUT NOTICE.

INDEX

A

abdominal muscles 87
abductor longus 110
abductors 111
ability 19, 28, 46, 77, 79, 80, 87, 88, 94, 103
Achilles tendon 63, 72, 79, 84
acquired strength 54
adductor muscles 59
aerobics 52, 63
age 1, 10, 11, 13, 19-22, 24, 27, 30, 44, 46-48, 50, 51, 52, 53, 94
age eight 44, 51
age seven 51
agility 79, 94, 95
aids 72, 107, 108, 110
American Baseball Coaches Association 17
Anderson, Bob 56, 62
An In Depth Analysis of the Bench Press 96
angles 12, 13, 37, 98
ankle 63-65, 72, 84, 85
anterior deltoid 56, 57, 91, 102, 107
anterior deltoid stretch 56
arc 14, 15
Arizona Republic 30
arm 1-3, 7, 9-17, 19-21, 27, 31, 32, 35, 38-42, 44-47, 50, 55, 57-60, 62, 69-71, 73, 75-78, 85-88, 90-93, 99, 100, 103-106, 108-111
atrocities 30
autonomic nervous system 79

B

Babe Ruth 10
backward spin 34
ball 1, 2, 10-17, 20, 22-24, 26-41, 43, 44, 46-48, 50, 51, 55, 56, 73, 74, 78, 94, 107-110
ball and socket 50
ball, transfer 22
barbell 70-72, 76-78, 83, 84, 86, 87, 90, 95-97, 101, 102, 103, 106
base coaches 31
baseball 1, 2, 9-11, 13, 17, 21-24, 26, 29, 30, 33, 43, 46, 48, 51, 52, 58, 63, 70, 75, 76, 80, 85, 88, 100, 108
baseball pitching 11, 13
baseballers 68
batter off balance 44
batting warm ups 56
Beginning Weight Training For Young Athletes 52, 68
behavior 24, 40
Bernoulli's law 34
biceps 57, 59, 77, 91, 92
biggest kid 47
biological clock 52
blind pitch 2
Black, Joe 42 body coordination 10, 32
body fatigue 46
body protection 50
body torque 33
bone 13, 14, 50, 55, 59
bone joint 55
Book of Stretching 56, 62
bring in 26
Brooklyn Dodgers 42
Bryant, Ron 14

C

calcified 11
calf and knee tendons 61
calf stretch 62
calves 74, 79

capillaries 11
Carlton, Steve 35, 41
carpi extensors/flexors 111
cartilage 11, 50
catcher 1, 2, 22, 26, 27, 36
centrifugal force 10
change-up 23, 33, 37, 44
cheap training 39, 107, 108
circuiting 73
clinic 21, 104
co-educational 68
coach and train 46
cold 55
coming around 74
concentration of effort 97
concerns 51
conditioning 11, 30, 54, 56, 63, 68, 80, 85, 96, 105, 110
conditioning stretches 23, 33, 37, 39, 40, 56
connective tissue 11, 55, 66, 72
continuum of socialization 52
controlling the program 48
coordination 10, 32, 51, 71, 73, 75, 92, 107
count 31, 42, 69
crowd the plate 24
cuff of tendon 14
cupping the hand 14
curve 11-15, 17, 23, 39, 54
curveball 2, 11, 13-15, 17, 18, 20, 27, 35, 38-41

D

de-rotates 15
de-rotation 17, 19
defensive strategies 27
deflated ego 45
delivery 2, 9, 10, 12-17, 22, 46, 55
delivery, 3/4 arm 12
delivery, improper 10
delivery, new 16, 17
delivery, pull down 16
deltoid(s) 9, 56-59, 60, 69, 71, 72, 76, 82, 91, 92, 94, 97, 100, 102, 103, 105, 106, 107

demanding pitches 38 development, ages 50-54
developmental stages 11, 30
dip 27
direction 7, 15, 39, 73, 109
donut 56
downward swing 14, 15
drills 32

E

effective leader 9, 11, 24, 40, 50, 77, 82, 89, 103, 106, 110, 111
elementary 2, 19, 20
endurance 54, 70, 82, 94, 95
epiphysis 9-11, 13, 27, 46, 50, 53, 55, 69-75, 77, 78, 80, 82-92, 97-103, 106, 107, 109
exercise(s) 11, 27, 53-56, 67, 69-75, 77, 78, 80, 83-92, 97-107, 109-111
expectations 47, 52
extensor carpi radialis longus 103
extensor exercise 98
extensors 78, 105, 109, 111
external obliques 9, 58, 74, 101

Face, Elroy 42
fastball 18, 22-24, 27, 33-37, 39-44
fat 52
fatal inside twist 12
Feldman, Jay 13-15, 17
Feller, Bob 1, 2
femoris muscle group 62
fibers 80, 104, 106
field position 47
finger placement 20
finger pressure 12, 13, 34-36, 39-41
firm contact 39
first batter, tactics 31
flexor 78, 86, 98, 106, 109, 110
forearm(s) 71, 76, 100, 103, 106
free weights 84
front press 90

front shoulder 56, 57, 91, 97, 102, 107
fuller movement 90
fun and fitness 51
fundamentals 32

G

game of averages 24
gastrocnemius 63
giving away the pitch 22
gluteal-spinal stretch 60
gluteus maximus 57
go wild 31
grip 22, 24, 34-36, 39, 41, 78, 88, 109, 110

H

hamstring spinal stretch 61
hamstrings 60, 61, 65, 66, 72, 74, 79
handball 11
has-beens 10, 19
Herzog, Whitey 28, 46
hide the ball 22, 31 high reps 70, 76
high school student 20
hinge joint 50
hips 52
hit 2, 3, 20, 23, 24, 27, 29-31, 36, 40, 46, 47, 56, 82, 94, 96, 107
hitting 28, 33, 36, 40, 51, 67, 71, 88, 110
Hodges, Gil 23, 26, 28, 29, 31, 41
How to Coach, Manage and Play Little League 26
humeral head 14
humerus 13, 14
hurdler stretch 55, 63, 64, 65
hyper-extension 63
hyperextended 86

I

improper 10, 61, 63-65
improper stretches 63
incorrect technique 62
index finger 14, 34, 36, 37, 40, 41

insensitive coach 52
inside fastball 33
Inside Hitting 33
inside pitch 33
instructor 1, 10, 48, 52, 61, 94-96
interest 51, 94
into the pitch 74

J

Jackson, Reggie 33
John C. Lincoln Hospital's Sports Medicine Clinic 104
joint(s) 9, 11, 14, 50, 53, 55, 69, 73, 77, 86, 89
joint capsule 50
jump rope 79, 80, 93, 103

K

knee, misalignment 66
knuckleball 43, 44

L

lactic acid 46
latissimus dorsi 9, 57, 59, 82, 89, 97, 100, 101
Lavelle, Gary 17
lazy glove arm 32
lead arm 32
lead foot 32
left-hander 36
ligament(s) 11, 61, 66, 69, 85, 104
line drive 3, 22
Little League 10, 11, 19, 21, 24, 26-29, 44, 45, 53, 110, 111
Little League elbow 110, 111
low strikes 31
lower triceps 69
lubricating fluid 50
lumbar 9, 57, 59, 96, 97

M

Mack, Connie 10

Maitland Sports Training 3, 11, 34, 56
managers 27
mature pitchers 40
maturity 40, 44, 50, 51, 53
Mays, Willie 29 meat of the bat 31
mechanical linkage 15
medial deltoid 72
membrane 50
menstruation 52
mental training 68
middle finger 34, 36, 40, 41
minor pectoralis 58, 81, 92
modify 94
momentum 13, 15
muscle,(s) 14, 17, 38, 46, 50, 53-63, 65-67, 69, 70-78, 80-83, 85-91, 94, 95, 97, 98, 100, 104, 106, 109, 110
muscling the ball 44
myth 14

N

National Strength and Conditioning Association 54, 63, 80, 96, 105
natural arm movement 19
natural rotation 15, 16
Niekro, Phil and Joe 43, 44
new delivery 16, 17
non-throwing arm 32
NSCA Journal 96

O

Olympic Fitness Equipment 83
opposing muscle 61, 86, 98
out front 14
outside corner pitch 33
over the shoulder delivery 12
over this head 51
overextension 77
overhand throwing 15
overhead wind-up 1, 7
overstraining 70, 82, 89
overthrow 31

overtiring 75, 100
overuse 44, 47
overzealous 10, 38
overzealous coaches 38

P

parents 3, 11, 13, 19-22, 28, 38, 45, 47, 49, 66, 107
patella 63, 83, 84, 86
patellar ligaments 61, 66
patellar tendons 63, 64, 83, 85
pectoralis 58, 59, 69, 76, 81, 82, 91, 92, 97, 100
pectoralis major 81, 97, 100
pelvis 52
permanent blood vessels 11
physiological basis 21
pitcher 2, 7, 9-12, 14, 15, 17, 20-28, 30-33, 36, 38, 40, 42-47, 50, 53, 55, 67, 71
pitches 11, 13, 17, 20, 22, 23, 38, 42-46
pitches, demanding 38
pitches, hang 40
pitches, per game 46
pitching 47
pitching, baseball 11, 13 pitching from the full wind-up 31
pitching from the stretch 31
Pittsburgh Pirates 42
pivot foot 2, 9, 31, 32
plateau 51
plyometric 68, 80
point of concentration pitching 2, 7, 9, 12
point of pain 62
Pop Warner 63
posterior deltoid 57, 58
power 13, 19, 30, 37, 67, 71, 74, 75, 77, 78, 82, 89, 94, 95
power finger 37
pre-season 13, 21, 110
pre-training warm ups and stretches 66
pressure 46
pressure, tendons 63, 64
pressure points 34, 35, 40
Program One 68

Program Two 67, 68
Program III 68
pronation of adductors 110
proper rest between games 44
puberty 52, 53
pulling down 14, 40

Q

quadriceps stretch 61, 62
quick strength 79, 83

R

racquetball 11, 44
Ramey, Melvin 15
range of motion 108
rapid development 79
rear deltoids 97
rear press 90
recruit 46
rectus abdominis 9
relationships 51
relaxed wrist 39
release 14-16, 35
relief pitchers 42
reps 69, 70, 72, 73, 76, 82, 85, 90, 94, 110
resistance 70, 88, 104
resting 45, 86, 110
rhomboid 72, 101
rhythm 7
right-hander 36
rise 34, 37, 90, 102
rising fastball 34, 35, 37, 41
Roman chair 87, 88
rookie league 17
rope jumping 93
rotate, arm 15, 90, 91
rotator cuff 9, 11, 13, 14, 17, 27, 46, 50, 69, 97, 106, 108-110
rotator cuff injuries 13, 14 rubber 9, 31
run in place 79

S

safe delivery 12
safe pitch 16
safe throwing habits 21
San Francisco Giants 14
sandlot ball 1, 47
scapular 72, 76, 82, 101
scout 28
screwball 27
Seaver, Tom 30-33, 36, 39, 40
sense of humor 48
sets of repetitions 69
shoulder injuries 19
shoulders 16, 52, 69-72, 75, 76, 84, 87, 88, 94, 97, 99, 100, 103
shrugs 73
sidearm 12, 13, 27
sinker 36, 37
sinking fastball 36
skills training 47
slider(s) 38, 40, 41
slump 31
snap 7, 35, 109
soccer 51
soleus 61
Solis, Victor, Jr. 48
sore arm 45
speed 7, 13, 14, 23, 30, 33, 34, 37, 39, 44, 70, 74, 76, 79, 95, 98
speed, change 33, 44
speed pitch 37, 39
sphere of influence 21
spin 2, 34, 35, 37
spinae erectors 59, 73, 74, 87
spinae flexors 71, 76, 101
spinal column 9, 61, 66, 74
spinal column stretch 66
spinning the ball 16
spinoff point 13
split finger fastball 18, 42-44
spotted 84
sprain 62
sprint machine 83

squat 70, 74, 75, 90
St. Louis Cardinals 28, 46
stabilization 62
stance 2, 9, 33, 39
standard method 11
sternum 96
stomach muscles 9, 58
straight fastballs 36
straight wrist 39
strain 27, 32, 54, 55, 57, 62, 84, 86, 97, 103, 104, 106, 109
straining 54, 75, 77, 100
strategy 27, 45
strength 2, 9, 19, 20, 30, 44, 52-54, 63, 71, 73, 76, 77, 79-83, 85-88, 92, 94-96, 99, 103, 105, 106, 108-110
strengthening 11, 17, 67, 72, 75, 83, 105, 106, 110, 111
stress 13, 16, 45, 62, 65, 66, 92, 111
stress, unnecessary emotional 45
stretch(es) 9, 31, 48, 55-66, 68, 69, 74, 80, 82, 84, 85-87, 89, 107, 109
stretching, improper 61
stride foot 2
strike zone 24, 27, 40
structure 13, 46, 50, 53
style of pitches 22, 43
subjective method 108
submariner pitch 18
supporting connective tissue 66
supporting ligaments 11
supportive 47
supraspinatus 14
Sutton, Don 2
Swimley, Phil 13
swing 14, 15, 33, 39, 107
swurve 12, 13, 37
systemic 46

T

tactics, first batter 31
T-Ball 30, 38, 51
T-Bench 106

teaching mind control 24
team 3, 21, 23, 24, 26, 28, 30, 31, 43, 46, 48, 51, 58
team sports 51
tendon(s) 14, 61, 62-66, 72, 79, 83-86, 104, 111
tennis 10, 11, 44
tennis ball 10
teres minor 14
The Art of Pitching 30, 32
The Game of Baseball 23
therapeutic 62, 104, 106, 108
therapeutic value 62, 106
therapy aids 107
thinking ballplayer 21
thinking pitcher 21, 24
threads 12, 13, 34, 37
throwing arm 32
throwing motion 109
thumb pad 39
tibia 64
tibial tendons 65, 66
tired 36, 46
tiring 70
tissue(s) 11, 50, 55, 66, 72
tissue, weakening 66 Today Show 46
torque 7, 9, 15, 33, 46
total athlete 11, 45
total ballplayer 28
total body involvement 22, 23
total condition 46
total muscle body 46
training 3, 11, 16, 19, 20, 22, 23, 30, 32, 44, 47-49, 52-56, 66-68, 70, 71, 76, 80, 82, 94, 98, 103, 106-110
trapezius 60, 72, 76, 97, 101
triceps 58, 59, 69, 77, 103, 105
trunk and shoulder stretch 57
twisting the arm 11

U

uncontrollable power in the throw 19
uninformed coaches 44

V

vastus medialis 62, 63
velocity 7, 9, 34
vertebrae 95, 96
vital organs 50

W

warm-up stretching 62
weight lifting 19, 95
weight training 3, 11, 19, 20, 22, 30, 32, 48, 52-56, 58, 67, 68, 94, 103, 110
weights 19, 23, 56, 70, 72, 76, 82, 84, 85, 90, 92, 98, 99
whipping motion 13
Wilhelm, Coit 42
wind-up stretch @INDEX PRIMARY = 58
World Series 42
wrist(s) 35, 39, 59, 69, 71, 73, 75, 76, 78, 82, 86, 88, 91, 92, 98, 99, 100, 105, 108, 109, 110, 111
wrist twist 69, 88

Y

young athletes 3, 11, 16, 18, 19, 46, 52, 63, 68, 83, 94, 96
young pitchers 2, 11, 14, 20, 22, 24, 30, 35, 40
youth league 21, 26, 46

CURRENT BOOKS AVAILABLE BY WILLIAM J. MAITLAND

WEIGHT TRAINING FOR GIFTED ATHLETES-150 pages-photos-ISBN#0-936-759-01-1 — Paperback
This book discusses the latest methods of training athletes ages 14 thru adult. Methods include PLYOMETRICS-WEIGHT TRAINING for recreational, amateur and professional athletes-NUTRITION-PHYSIOLOGICAL and PSYCHOLOGICAL DEVELOPMENT of the growing mind and body and proper STRETCHING techniques for boys and girls ages 14 through adult. $17.95 U.S. FUNDS RETAIL.

BEGINNING WEIGHT TRAINING FOR YOUNG ATHLETES-AGES 12 THRU ADULT-90 pages ISBN # 0-936-759-003 — Paperback $9.95 U.S. FINDS RETAIL-second printing-$14.95 U.S. FUNDS (when available).

An excellent book for the beginner of any age. Photos display each exercise in great detail and simplicity. Universities, Junior-high Schools, Sports Clinics and Sports Trainers all over the world have found this book useful in their programs of teaching students at all levels as future instructors-coaches of youngsters all over the world. The book contains nutrition information and the dangers of over-training for boys and girls.

Coach Maitland showing Matt Barclay a safe pitch.

Greg Paul at age 18
Weight Training Gifted Athletes

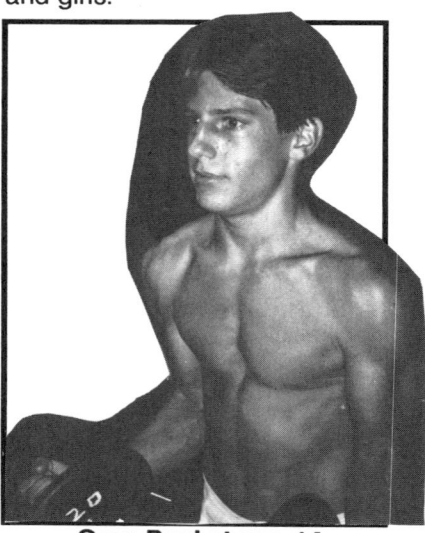

Greg Paul at age 14
Beginning Weight Training

YOUNG BALL PLAYERS GUIDE TO SAFE PITCHING - Ages 8 thru Adult (with weight training for developing **full body power**) - 130 pages — Paperback   ISBN 0-936759-14-3
$14.95 U.S..   Publish date 7-92

This book contains a new approach to pitching beginning at age eight. The young ballplayer is taught to use the powers of concentration along with the full use of the body for power delivery. The young ballplayer is taught the use of plyometric training in preparing for the pitch.

Weight training programs are included along with proper stretching methods. The young ballplayer learns to strengthen the entire body rather than relying on arm strength only. He/she is taught the value of strength and conditioning for baseball in all areas of the game.

Examples are shown in clear, concise, black and white photos of baseball pitching grips used in the games of the past as well as new grips that "move the ball" more efficiently with no strain on the young pitchers developing arm.

The author played ball since early childhood and continues to coach young pitchers at "MAITLAND'S SPORTS TRAINING" in Phoenix, Arizona. All Maitland's books are endorsed by Dr. Art Mollen for training safety and benefits to the developing young athletes, the books have endorsements from readers, trainers, schools and university coaches around the world. (ORDER FORM ON REVERSE SIDE)